God's Word:

Unique, Magnetic, Eternal

Norm Lewis

Foreword by
George Verwer

LITERATURE

GOD'S WORD: Unique, Magnetic, Eternal

Published by
OM Literature
P.O. Box 1047
Waynesboro, GA
30830-2047
USA
(706) 554-5827

ISBN 18845-4308-1

Printed by:
New Life Literature (pvt) Ltd.,
Spur Road 4, E.P.Z.
Katunayake, Sri Lanka.

Contents

Foreword, Author's Word

God's Word

Memorize to Obey God

Read to Obey God

Help from this Book? . . . How?

1. Embrace two BIBLE tasks: **MEMORIZE & READ**;

2. **Why?** In order **to OBEY God;**

3. Don't tackle both tasks at once. **Do memory discipline only for 40 days, see Caution! below;**

4. **Overlearn** each text before starting next;

5. **Review** every day;

6. **Share texts with believers, then with others.** You
   will use them, or lose them.

Caution!

My Bible memory work and ambitious Bible reading
as told in this book started seven years apart. Each was
tough, though the dividends were big!

And, "God is faithful. He will keep the temptation
from becoming so strong that you can't stand up against
it" (1 Cor.10:13 lnt). "God blesses people who patiently
endure testing" (Jas.1:12 lnt). The prize is great!

To win, you too will pay a price. It may cost you
radical changes in life style. It's a blood, sweat and tears
thing! So, think carefully about it. Don't underestimate
the task and risk defeat, for God's rewards for victory
are huge!

It is **not** wise to launch into both memorizing and
reading disciplines at the same time. Start the memory
work first, pages 37-84. After 40 days, when you are
used to the new rhythm, start ambitious Bible reading,
pages 85-90.

Foreword

I praise God for this biblical heartfelt plea for all of us to get into a more dynamic daily relation with the Bible.

Norm Lewis is a long-term spiritual marathon runner for the Kingdom of God. I count it a privilege to be linked with him for the past thirty-seven years.

I feel strongly that neglecting to read and meditate God's Word is the reason so many of God's people seem to be spiritually anemic. It is my prayer that those who read this book will be moved to find ways to share it widely with other believers. The need is enormous!

After my conversion I began to memorize the Bible and it was one of the most important factors in my early spiritual growth. All over the world I have urged people to meditate and memorize the Word of God.

I thank God for this book that will help people do just that. I hope you will follow the plan carefully. Read and memorize the Bible in order to obey God. Do it to live a transformed life!

—*George Verwer*

Our Greatest Asset

The Bible is our greatest human asset, the masterpiece of God. It comes to us drenched in the tears of millions of contritions, worn with the fingers of the saints of the ages, expounded by the greatest intellects, and stained with blood of the martyrs.

It is the fountain in which dying believers cooled their hot faces, the pillow on which saints of all ages rested their heads. It breaks the fetters of the slave, takes the heat out of life's fierce fever, the pain out of parting, the sting out of death and the gloom out of the grave.

The Bible is the old-time book, the new-time book, the all-time book. It will demonstrate its own character and its own power. This is the rock of all ages and they who build upon it are as eternal as God.

The name of Jesus, the Supreme Personality, the center of the world's desire is on every page in one form or another. Pierce the book anywhere and it will bleed with His priceless blood, shed for our redemption.

This divine book has all the answers to man's every need. To find them and share them with everyone everywhere, both in our Jerusalem, Judea, Samaria and to the farthest parts of earth is our greatest privilege and responsibility.

—Author unknown

Author's Word

This book offers you something very valuable. That treasure is in another Book. The reason for this book is that Book. This book tells how people like you found the Bible, or how the Bible found them. Think about today's Agony, its Blessings, and how you can be safe and secure at the Close of your life, a simple A, B, C.

Agony

Everything seems out of joint. People killing people. Ethnic cleansing, civilians driven from their homes, families slaughtered—men, women and children. Political entities powerless to stop the carnage. Government leaders widely in disrepute. Dysfunctional families. Over 50% of marriages fail. Workers hate bosses. One strike cost two billion dollars. What chaos!

Everything on earth is passing. Possessions we call ours are just "borrowed for a while." The items we prize most will belong to someone else. The place I once called home is now a vacant lot. The house was leveled by bulldozers, all is gone.

Yes, things are temporary. They can't be kept. The poet said, "They build too low who build beneath the stars." And Solomon, the most famous and powerful king in the world in his day said, "Vanity of vanities, all is vanity" (Eccl.1:1).

Blessings

People are important. "God so loved the world..."(Jn. 3:16). "He is not willing that any should perish" (2 Pet. 3:9).

Abraham understood and lived as a stranger in a foreign land. His eyes were on the city with foundations whose architect and builder is God. The Apostle Paul wrote, "If the earthly tent we live in is torn down, we know we'll get one from God, not made by human hands, but lasting forever in heaven " (2 Cor. 5:1 Beck).

Jesus said, "Do not lay up for yourselves treasures on earth... lay up for yourselves treasures in heaven, where neither moth nor rust destroys, where thieves do not break in and steal" (Mt. 6:19-).

Hope in Christ is permanent. You can have wealth, success, fame and power apart from God, but you cannot have hope. God by his grace chose believers as his very own, loved them and gave them eternal salvation. For that reason alone they have hope.

Paul speaks of "the hope of the gospel" (Col. 1:23), meaning the hope to see fulfilled all the promises given in the gospel. Apart from the gospel there is no hope. Three adjectives in the Bible describe our hope: "good, blessed, and living." (2 Thess. 2:16; Titus 2:13; and 1 Pet. 1:3). This hope is unique to the gospel.

When Dr. Samuel Johnson was nearly blind and tortured from illness, he wrote that human life is a struggle in which we move not from pleasure to pleasure, but from hope to hope.

Again Paul said, "May our Lord Jesus Christ himself and God our Father, who loved us and by his grace gave us eternal encouragement and good hope, encourage your hearts and strengthen you in every good deed and word" (2 Thess. 2:16- niv).

People long for life everlasting. Hope in Christ conquers death. Paul, in Romans, which has been called "the greatest message ever written by a man," says, "For whatever things were written before were written for our learning, that we through the patience and comfort of the Scriptures might have hope" (Rom. 15:4).

Close

"So I pray that God, who gives you hope, will keep you happy and full of peace as you believe in him. May you overflow with hope through the power of the Holy Spirit" (Rom.15:13 nlt).

James Dobson said it well: "Do I, you ask, really believe in this 'hope of glory' beyond the grave for those who have been covered with the blood of the Lamb? You bet I do—with every fibre of my being! I have banked everything of value to me on that promise.

"Isaiah laid it out for us in plain terms: 'Yet we have this assurance: those who belong to God shall live again. Their bodies shall rise! Those who dwell in the dust shall awake and sing for joy! For God's light of life will fall like dew on them!'" (Isa. 26:19 tlb).

My wife's brother, Paul, himself a believer, told us in 1992 how shaken he had been by the tragic end of the lives of two of his best friends. All three were teachers at the Delgado Industrial School where Paul taught for 34 years. His fellow teachers both killed themselves. When people have no hope, everything is black.

Let this book nudge you toward the Bible which offers, in all God's universe, the only true hope. May your life's north star and your last words be, "My hope is built on nothing less, than Jesus blood and righteousness."

God's Word:
Unique

What do those three words signify? They mean one-of-a-kind. The Bible stands alone. To say of anything, "It is very unique," is incorrect. Uniqueness signifies a category by itself in which the subject cannot be compared with anything which is said to resemble it, for that would invalidate its uniqueness.

Thus anything unique cannot be compared with similar things because there are no such. It is incomparable. The Bible is unique.

It was written by some forty different human authors over a period of 1500 years. What other book can be compared to it in the number of its authors? Yet its consistency is amazing. Has any book in history been produced by such a diversity of authors? It is unique.

And what about the huge span of time invested in its production? How would you feel if asked to write something to be part of a book started in 998 A.D.? Or even in 1298 A.D.? Who would guide such a project?

Corporations today boast of having a history of 50, 70, or 100 years. But how many businesses can boast of 500 or 1000 years of existence? The Bible is unique in the time that spanned its production..

Yet the Bible unfolds a plan which is coherent, systematic and all-inclusive. It is God's plan for the redemption of our race through Jesus Christ. It embraces the future of every person on this planet. The Bible is unique in its plan.

What shall we say about the Bible's capacity to capture men of the most diverse and unlikely sorts? This book contains such accounts. These men were not religious; God reached them through a Book. Yet their commitment was permanent. The Bible is unique in its power.

What invisible fascination drew Baltadono that life-changing day and night? (See page 23). Or Avellaneda? (See page 13). Or Cailliet? (See page 27). To what other book do people respond in such a way? Unwavering. The Bible is unique in its magnetism.

The Apostle Peter touches the felt need of every pilgrim on earth for something that will last. Nice, but temporary, sums up every human dream and plan.

Peter says, "All flesh is as grass, and all the glory of man as the flower of the grass. The grass withers, and its flower falls away, But the word of the Lord endures forever. Now this is the word which by the gospel was preached to you" (1 Pet.1:24-) The Bible is unique in its eternal relevance.

The Bible leads the way in elevating humanity. Wherever it goes it liberates slaves, betters the condition of women, builds hospitals, and in other ways lifts humanity. The Bible is unique in its empowering.

It sends a man like Charles Colson into the prisons of the world and in a few years a host of advocates are seeking to improve the plight of men and women behind bars. What other book so motivates people? The Bible is unique in its influence..

Why do men recognize its authority over their lives? What happened to Donald G. Barnhouse (See page 31)? What caused that gifted man to recognize in a flash the enormous difference between the Bibles's print and newsprint? This Book is unique in its authority.

Bible prophesies reveal a knowledge of future events that denies any explanation except divine foresight. Of the more than 1000 forecasts of specific coming occurrences in God's Word, more than 650 have been verified by history. None have been disproved. The Bible is unique in the accuracy of its prophesies.

Pascal's Wager

Avoid spiritual indifference. Fight apathy. They drown people in a sea of trivia and rob them of desire to find God. To read, memorize and meditate the Bible will move you toward Him. Blaise Pascal (1623-1662) somehow knew that.

He was born in France, his father a government official. His mother died when he was three years old. Blaise was a mathematical genius, a physicist, and an amazing biblical thinker. He was fascinated by scientific studies. At 19 he began work on a calculating machine, the father of the computer.

His father died in 1651; two years later, Blaise at 31 was converted. Through that experience his mind flamed with the conviction of being overwhelmed by light. He knew "joy, joy, joy, tears of joy," and was transported to a new level of "certitude, heartfelt joy, and peace."

Pascal lived deeply in the Bible, especially in Psalm 119, which lifted him to ecstasy. His physical pain and weakness increased, yet during the remaining eight short years of his life he produced his *Pensees.*

Pascal opened himself in prayer to God's scrutiny. His worship was as secret as his prayer, Bible reading, and giving. "According to his family, he literally knew the Bible by heart."[1]

Pascal deplored the apathy and indifference which cause people to fritter away their lives in meaningless trifles, with no seeming concern for the eternity to which they go. In the "Wager" which follows, Pascal invites us, saying,

"Let us weigh the gain and the loss in wagering that God is. Let us estimate these two chances. If you gain, you gain all; if you lose, you lose nothing. Wager then without hesitation that God is."

Pascal's argument can be reduced to four propositions:

1. If I believe and I am right, when I die, I gain everything.
2. If I believe and I am wrong, when I die (if death is the end of all things), I lose nothing.
3. If I disbelieve and I am right, when I die (if death is the end of all things), I gain nothing.
4. If I disbelieve and I am wrong, when I die (since death is not the end of all things), I lose everything.

Conclusions:
1. I have everything to gain by belief, nothing to lose; I have nothing to gain by unbelief but everything to lose.
2. On this wager the stakes are extremely high. I am not betting dollars and cents. I am wagering my life and eternity.
3. **The wager is not an argument for belief. It proves nothing. It is rather an argument against my unbelief or apathy as to making a full commitment to Christ. That stance is not tenable. Unbelief has nothing to sustain it.[2]**

"Kid" Avellaneda

It was after midnight in the dark pavilions of the 80 year old prison in Rosario, Argentina. The year was 1951. Aided by a dim light, one of the convicts, Jose "Kid" Avellaneda, was reading a New Testament in his cell. Hardly a case for conversion!

Born some 35 years previously, the illegitimate son of a priest, the baby was given away to hide the sin. Avellaneda's childhood was blows and bitterness. For years he had no name. His present name was given him by the justice of the peace who registered him as an Argentine citizen.

He remembers many beatings but never a mother's kiss. Hating and hated he came to consider society the author of all his tragedies. A career of crime seemed life's only course. His natural ability called him to the attention of other criminals. He became the leader of a band of delinquents.

Twenty checkered years followed. Kid Avellaneda's reputation grew. He gambled, was a card shark, won horse racing swindles, and organized similar activities. He posed as a doctor, and later as a lawyer. Thus he gained access to wealthy and influential people.

Prison sentences were short until 1945. Then the theft of a million and a half pesos in tires and automobiles put him behind bars for ten years. In prison he educated himself, reading widely: Freud, Kant, Schopenhauer, Aristotle, and others. Through the mail he received a New Testament. He began to read it. Then a miracle took place.

That never-to-be-forgotten night, as Avellaneda read of Christ's crucifixion between two thieves, his hard heart broke. Sobbing he flung himself to his knees beside the iron cot. When day came, Jose was a new man. His was a Saul of Tarsus conversion.

The change in his conduct was startling. He ceased to hate. He sought to fulfill every assigned task. Prison authorities, gradually convinced of his changed character, gave Avellaneda special liberties.

He was promoted to secretary in the prison office. At certain hours he was permitted to leave the prison. Not once did he violate the confidence placed in him. In 1952 prison officials sought his pardon. Avellaneda was free.

But the battle had just begun. Work was impossible to find. This child of God could not conceal his past. In every application for work he stated he had been a criminal for twenty yeas. Would-be employers read no further! Every door closed. Avellaneda had married a humble Christian girl. How they suffered! Starvation threatened.

His old gang tempted him with offers of big money in crime. Faith wavered but did not fail. Gradually Jose learned to sell. Thus he provided a living for his wife and two children. Later he and his wife joined the church I pastored in Rosario, Argentina. A year of almost daily fellowship followed.

When Avellaneda left Rosario, it was to accept the pastorate of a small church in Buenos Aires. His ministry continued in Argentine prisons.

The transformation of Jose Avellaneda must have an explanation. I believe it was the love of God that worked in his life. I saw it myself. I was a witness.

What book besides the Bible could change such a man? God's Word is unique in its power to transform lives. Do you want God to work in your life? Do you want to be God's agent to accomplish what He wants in others?

Truth does wonders. God's Word memorized, read and meditated in order to obey God is His answer. He will lead you to pray, live by faith, be filled with His Spirit, witness, and be more than a conqueror through Him.

Fit for a King

The Bible was written by men who "spoke as they were moved by the Holy Spirit" (2 Pet.1:21). The Spirit reveals God's purpose that the believer should depend on the Bible and the Spirit to know what he must be and do to obey God.

The prophet Samuel had been Israel's spiritual leader for many years. One day the elders of Israel said to him, "Look, you are old, and your sons do not walk in your ways. Now make us a king to judge us like all the nations" (1 Sam. 8:5). Amazingly, their sacred Scripture, written generations earlier, profiled their king:

"It shall be, when he sits on the throne of his kingdom, that he shall write for himself a copy of this law in a book...

"It shall be with him, and he shall read it all the days of his life, that he may learn to fear the Lord his God and be careful to observe all the words of this law...

"That his heart may not be lifted above his brethren, that he may not turn aside from the commandment to the right hand or to the left and that he may prolong his days in his kingdom..." (Deut. 17:18-20).

How amazing! Notice:

1. **"He shall write for himself a copy of this law in a book."** He had to copy the Scriptures, for it was essential that he have God's Book, as the ruler of God's people.
2. **"It shall be with him,"** kept close for ready reference. Only God's Book could meet the king's needs.
3. **"He shall read it all the days of his life."** For him to read the Bible daily was God's clear command. A permanent order, for life!
4. **"That he may learn to fear the Lord his God."** Fear of the Lord" was and is, a learned attitude.
5. **"Be careful to observe all the words of this law."** Why? "All Scripture is inspired by God and is profitable," i.e., useful, practical (2 Tim. 3:16).
6. **"That his heart may not be lifted above his brethren."** God's Word combats the awful sin of pride.

7. **"That he may not turn aside from the commandment
   to the right hand or the left."** To obey God was non-
   negotiable then and now. Bible-in-the-heart was needed in
   order to walk in obedience to God.

8. **"That he may prolong his days in his kingdom, he
   and his children in the midst of Israel."** Obedience
   through reading God's Word would lengthen his life and
   the lives of his children

Remember, the quoted words are from the Bible. How could the
need for daily intake of God's Word be more strongly stated?

God's intent has always been the same: that people should
willingly obey Him. What is more important than that? It is a non-
negotiable priority.

To neglect God's Word will be more costly than anyone can
know.

Hsi, a witness

For three years North China was devastated by terrible famine. Need created opportunity, and a group of missionaries penetrated to Shansi in order to distribute famine relief to the starving multitudes.

In order to make an approach to the scholar class one of them, David Hill, offered a prize for the best essay written in classical style. When the essays were submitted one of them was outstanding, and its author was informed that he had won the prize.

He was so bitterly opposed to the foreigner, his religion and all his ways, that he sent his brother-in-law to claim the money, but when this relative came he was politely informed by David Hill that the silver could only be handed to the writer himself.

After performing many idolatrous rites to make sure no demon could hurt him, scholar Hsi presented himself to the foreigner who gave him the money. Not until later did David Hill suggest that Hsi should teach him, and only under stress of dire poverty did this very proud Chinese consent to come into such close contact with a foreigner.

David Hill never in any way pressed Christianity upon his teacher, who was left free to write in his own room, to take his periodical dose of opium, and to hold himself aloof from the missionary's evangelistic work. He had, however, daily opportunity of meeting the missionary himself and he formed his own opinion about him: "A princely man," was his inner Confucian verdict on Dad Hill.

There was a New Testament in Chinese in the study where he worked, and one day he opened it and began to read about this Jesus, who, though He went about doing good, was killed by evil men. As he read and reread the story it came alive, he saw the Lord, and with tears he knelt and yielded himself unreservedly to His service.

The Bible had done its own work and through it the Holy Spirit had revealed Christ to this man whose mind had been filled with violent prejudice against Western religions, and with a determination to have nothing to do with them.

The printed Book, illustrated by the living actions of the missionary, demanded a verdict, and that verdict produced the total change of outlook which we call conversion.

New life began at once. He cut all idolatrous practices and spent hours reading the New Testament, which he took as literal instructor in every department of life. The Book reshaped the life of the Confucian scholar, who became a great Christian force in his native province.

He began his spiritual pilgrimage as a drug addict, but he soon came to recognize that opium-smoking was not merely an evil habit, but a satanic tyranny over the soul which could only be broken by the power of Christ, and fought with spiritual weapons.

He would not even compromise with the enemy to the extent of taking a graduated dose according to accepted medical treatment. He preferred the courageous step of smashing his pipe and trusting God to set him free from sin.

It was done, and the man with a new name, Hsi Sheng-mo (Overcomer of Demons), saw the first of many demons put under his feet. In time he established a number of opium refuges by means of which many drug addicts were led to Christ.[3]

—Cable and French

God's Word: Magnetic

The magnetic quality of the Bible is unrivaled. This book contains examples. What explains its strange ability to draw such diverse and unlikely men to its pages? And having captured their attention, what holds them in its power? Consider some amazing consequences of that magnetism.

How can one account for the totally unexpected transformation of Jose Avellaneda (see page 13) in prison in Argentina? From what source came the sudden love for righteousness in a man who had known only criminal activity since childhood?

Or what of the Chinese scholar Hsi (see page 17), saturated with bitter contempt for all foreigners and anything associated with them? From whence came the revolution in his life and conduct, which he formerly would have died to avoid? What produced the change?

What gave its strange appeal to Bunyan's *Pilgrim's Progress*, second in circulation only to the Bible which inspired it and to which it pointed? How explain its vast appeal and readership? One would hardly consider a 17th century English prison the place to produce an all-time best-seller. Yet Bunyan's book has impacted the lives of countless readers worldwide.

The phenomenon we call magnetism has interesting qualities. Magnetic fields both attract and repel. This is also true of the Bible. Wherever it goes, it polarizes people. Some it draws irresistibly and others it offends. Nor does the Bible leave us untaught concerning the reason for this property.

Jesus says clearly, "All things have been delivered to Me by My Father, and no one knows the Son except the Father. Nor does anyone know the Father except the Son, and the one to whom the Son wills to reveal Him" (Mt. 11:27).

Unless the Bible draws you powerfully, the Lord Jesus has apparently not seen in you a willingness to come. This conclusion seems valid because His invitations are universal with no hint of rejecting anyone wanting to come.

Strange, is it not, that His, "Come to me all you who labor and are heavy laden, and I will give you rest" (Mt. 11:28) follows immediately the truth of Mt. 11:27 just noted?

This invitation was as much to any stranger in the crowd as to

Jesus' followers. It shut out neither friend nor enemy. Jesus loved sinners of every sort. For them He would die.

Again in John 6:37 God's Son brings together in one sentence the two basic truths, "All that the Father gives Me will come to Me, and the one who comes to Me I will by no means cast out" (Jn. 6:37).

Think also of Jesus' statement, "No one can come to Me unless the Father, who sent Me draws him; and I will raise him up at the last day" (Jn. 6:44).

Those solemn facts are reinforced by our Lord's words, "But there are some of you who do not believe." For Jesus knew from the beginning who they were who did not believe, and who would betray Him. And He said, "Therefore I have said to you that no one can come to Me unless it has been granted to him by My Father" (Jn. 6:64-)

Even unbelief in harsh confrontation did not upset Jesus. He answered, "If anyone hears My words and does not believe, I do not judge him; for I did not come to judge the world but to save the world. He who rejects Me, and does not receive My words, has that which judges him—the word that I have spoken will judge him in the last day.

"For I have not spoken on my own authority; but the Father who sent Me gave Me a command, what I should say and what I should speak. And I know that His command is everlasting life. Therefore, whatever I speak just as the Father has told Me, so I speak" (Jn. 12:47-).

The above words should send you to the Bible. Read the Gospel of John. Read it with an open heart. Ask yourself whether the events seem caused by merely human sources. Or does the Bible have a higher origin?

John said, "Jesus' disciples saw him do many other miraculous signs besides the ones recorded in this book. But these are written so that you may believe that Jesus is the Messiah, the Son of God, and that by believing in him you will have life" (Jn. 20:30-).

Indicating how he was going to die, Jesus himself said, "And when I am lifted up on the cross, I will draw everyone to myself" (Jn. 12:32 nlt). May you yield to the Bible's tug toward Him.

Bunyan, a witness

Pilgrim's Progress by John Bunyan "has been printed, read and translated more often than any book other than the Bible." What magnetism! What would draw so vast a multitude of readers? The author was saturated with the Book! *Pilgrim's Progress* breaths the fragrance of the Bible.

Bunyan was born in 1628 in the village of Elstow, England. At 19 he married an orphan who was a praying Christian. She led him to the Lord and he was baptized. Bunyan began to preach but was arrested and imprisoned for preaching without permission from the Established Church.

His prison term lasted twelve years, during which time he wrote *Pilgrim's Progress,* from which the following is taken:

"I dreamed a Dream…and behold I saw a Man cloathed with rags, standing in a certain place…a Book in his hand, and a great Burden upon his back. I looked, and saw him open the book, and read therein; and as he read, he wept and trembled.

"Not being able longer to contain, he brake out with a lamentable cry, saying, What shall I do?" He tried in vain to warn his family. He then met Evangelist who gave him a Roll (Bible). In it he found, "Fly from the Wrath to come" (Mt. 3:7).

Heavily burdened, he started his journey. When asked, how did you get your burden? He answered, "By reading this book in my hand." Fearful because of warnings from two false friends, "he felt in his bosom for his Roll (Book) that he might read therein and be comforted; but he felt, and found it not. Then was Christian in great distress…"

After asking God's forgiveness for foolishly losing his Book, he went back to look for it. "Carefully looking on this side and on that, all the way as he went, if happily he might find the Roll that had been his comfort so many times in his journey.

"At last he spied it, the which he with trembling and haste catched up and put into his bosom. But who can tell how joyful this man was when he had gotten his Roll again, for in it was the Assurance of his Life, and Acceptance at the desired Haven."[4]

To read the Bible in truth means to let the Bible read you. To have one's heart searched daily by the Bible is one of the best gifts God has given our race. To obey the Spirit's guidance means life, the "more abundant life" which Jesus promised.

No such leading is possible for the one who lacks the Bible. That person is in darkness. Apart from the Bible one cannot obey "every word of God" (Lk. 4:4). Apart from the Bible there is no viable future for our race.

Thus John Bunyan confirms the importance of Bible reading. It is not an option; no acceptable choice exists. God's guidance alone can meet our need.

The world's utmost tragedy is humanity's rejection of God's way. The vast majority of earth's people have lost their Roll (Bible). The long slide to judgment continues. Our world's doom is sealed. In Jesus' own word picture of our day, the people say, "We will not have this man (Jesus) to rule over us" (Lk. 19:14).

To what will this lead? Paul tells us, "Then the lawless one will be revealed whom the Lord will consume with the breath of His mouth and destroy with the brightness of His coming.

"The coming of the lawless one is according to the working of Satan, with all power, signs, and lying wonders, and with all unrighteous deception among those who perish, because they did not receive the love of the truth, that they might be saved.

"And for this reason God will send them strong delusion, that they should believe the lie, that they all may be condemned who did not believe the truth but had pleasure in unrighteousness" (2 Thess. 2:8-).

Why is mercy's door still open? God's grace alone explains it. Do not presume. God's Word declares that "as many as receive Jesus Christ, to them He gives the right to become children of God, to those who believe in His name" (Jn. 1:12).

Baltadono, a witness

In Argentina, in 1947, I met a man named Baltadono. He was from Bolivia and told me about his life. Baltadono said that when he was a boy, a man came through his Bolivian village in 1905 selling Bibles and New Testaments. Baltadono bought a little black pocket edition of the New Testament with Psalms.

Next day the church bell began to ring wildly and the village people rushed there as was their custom, to see what was the matter. The priest told the villagers that an evil man had been among them selling a bad book called the Bible, and that all the Bibles must be destroyed. Baltadono went home, took the New Testament, put it on the top of a large wardrobe and there it stayed for several years.

Baltadono by this time had taken up smoking, One day he came home and found he had no cigarette paper. Searching for a substitute, he remembered the little book he had bought. He took it from the top of the wardrobe and tore out the first page.

Carefully he rolled the leaf tobacco in his hand, broke it up, put it on the paper, and rolled the cigarette. The fine paper made a very good cigarette, and so from that time he continued to use the New Testament, page by page for that purpose.

One day he tore a page from the Testament, rolled the tobacco, and was ready to drop it on the paper when his eye caught the words, "The Son of Man is come to seek and save that which was lost."

Baltodono laid down the tobacco and read the rest of the page. He turned it over and read the other side. He then picked up the New Testament and read on. Finally he had to get up and light two candles as night came on and he was still reading.

The candles burned low and had to be replaced. But Baltadono kept reading on through the night. At last — he told me — just as the eastern sky began to glow with the light of dawn, he got out of his chair, knelt down, put his face in his hands, and asked Christ to come into his heart and forgive his sins.

That morning, after breakfast, he continued to be amazed at the wonderful story in the little black book. Baltadono got what money he had and started the long hike to a larger village some kilometers away. There he was able to buy another Testament. He was determined to read the part of the book he had smoked up, Matthew,

Mark, and eighteen chapters of Luke.

His interest in God's Word continued. He began to testify, then to preach. Later he was able to buy a Bible. Truth had captured Baltadono when he providentially exposed himself to it. He was drawn irresistibly by its fascinating power.

The more he understood the teachings of the Bible, the more he felt empowered to share them for he discovered that they met human needs. His preaching improved. He kept sharing the wonderful truths he discovered as the years passed.

When he told me his story in 1947, he was helping missionaries from abroad understand the culture and language of Argentina. He confessed freely that the little black book he had bought as a lad in his remote Bolivian village had changed his character and outlook forever.

It was some time after Baltadono found forgiveness through Christ that to his surprise and delight he discovered other believers. He was not alone in the world! Others, too, had a vital relationship with the living God.

God's Word had transformed Baltadono. Amazing reality!

Sure Cure

"How can a young man cleanse his way? By taking heed according to Your word.

With my whole heart I have sought You; oh, let me not wander from Your commandments!

Your word I have hidden in my heart, that I might not sin against You." (Psa. 119:9-)

Eat More Bible

God's Word says people need more than physical food; **real life comes by feeding on every word of the Lord"** (Deut. 8:3 nlt).

Get that! "Real life comes by feeding on every word of the Lord." Isn't that what you want? God Himself provides the only food which nourishes believers. His order to live "by every word of God" (Lk. 4:4) is as much a command as, "You shall have no other gods before Me" (Ex. 20:3).

Meaning? If you want spiritual life, receive Christ, then read and obey God's Word. Read it as often as you feed your body. Someone asks, "You mean three times a day?" Why not ?

Would you obey God if you knew it was the only way to keep the world from pressing you into its mold? That is probably true.

Spiritual calories are as essential for spiritual growth as physical calories are for bodily growth. Those who study nutrition have measured the number of calories needed for normal growth for babies, children, teens, adults, men, women, etc.

Countless believers who think they are following Christ are not receiving the Bible calories needed to grow. Some never have! Small wonder worldliness is common. Many are spiritually starved.

What about you? Could this be your problem? Don't compare yourself with other believers. God says that those who compare themselves among themselves are not wise. By His grace, the remedy is as close as your Bible. But you must set spiritual goals and pursue them.

Does spiritual growth result from joining a church? It may or may not. What produces spiritual growth? "Real life comes by feeding on every word of the Lord." Life is essential for growth. Live babies grow.

These facts emphasize that people need more than physical food; **"real life comes by feeding on every word of the Lord."**

God has told us to read and memorize His Word daily. Why? In order to obey Him. We must know and do what He wants. But that is is not natural to us.

The Bible says our heart is deceitful above all things. Our mind is flawed by sin. "The natural man does not receive the things of the Spirit of God, for they are foolishness to him" (1 Cor. 2:14).

The average person spends a third of his life sleeping. Many believers average no more than two or three hours a week in "spiritual activities." Nor are they feeding even that much time on "every word of God." The balance of more than 100 hours a week they swim in an ocean of culture. Why should they grow spiritually?

Jesus said, "It is written, Man shall not live by bread alone, but by every word of God" (Lk. 4:4). How much is it worth to you to live by "every word of God"?

God made the perfect food for His people forty years called manna. Our manna is "every word of God." How do we define "spiritual food"? Is our definition broader than God's? Does that explain our multitudes of weak believers?

Why did God send the manna? To teach that believers must live connected to Himself. **Jesus said, "I am the vine, you are the branches" (Jn. 15:5). "Real life comes by feeding on every word of the Lord" (Deut. 8:3).**

Imagine reading the Bible as often as you eat. What difference would it make? You are hungry, you eat and grow stronger. Feed your spirit more, you will be stronger spiritually.

Why not? The logic is simple. If Jesus tarries, we will all die. Our bodies will return to dust (Gen. 2:7; 3:19), but our spirits will live forever (Jn.10:27-). Spirit or body, which deserves most care? The spirit, for it will live eternally.

Are believers taught that? They should be. Most are spiritual babies, though they think they are mature. God's Word says, "Though by this time you ought to be teachers, you need someone to teach you again the first principles...You need milk and not solid food" (Heb. 5:12).

Who can deny that to feed our spirit as often as our body would please God? Paul said, "We make it our aim, whether present or absent, to be well pleasing to Him. For we must all appear before the judgment seat of Christ" (2 Cor. 5:9-).

And again, "Exercise yourself toward godliness. Godliness is profitable for ALL THINGS (emphasis mine), having promise of the life that now is, AND of that which is to come" (1 Tim. 4:7-).

Will you feed your spirit as it deserves? How else can you correct the imbalance practiced so long? Start today. One way is to read and pray to start the day, review memory texts at noon, read God's Word at night, and meditate yourself to sleep.

Cailliet, a witness

Through my   college days in France I was an agnostic. Strange as it may seen, I graduated without ever having seen a Bible...the education I received proved of little help through front line experiences as a lad of 20 in World War I...

What use...the philosophic banter of the seminar, when your own buddy—at the time speaking to you of his mother—dies standing in front of you, a bullet in his chest? Was there a meaning to it all? One night a bullet got me too. An American field ambulance saved my life and later restored the use of my left arm...

I was discharged and resumed graduate work. I found myself probing in depth for meaning. During long night watches, a few yards from the German trenches, I looked at swollen bodies dangling in the barbed wires,

I had been strangely longing for...a book that would understand me. But I knew of no such book. Now I would in secret prepare one for my own use. And so as I went on reading for my courses, I would file passages that spoke to my condition, then carefully copy them in a leather-bound pocket book I always carried with me.

The day came when I put the finishing touch to the "book that would understand me,"...and help me. A beautiful day! At last, I...opened my precious anthology.

As I went on reading, however, a growing disappointment came over me. Then I knew that the whole undertaking would not work, simply because it was of my own making.

At that moment my British born wife—who knew nothing of my project—appeared. (I had once for all made the subject of religion taboo in our home.)

(Note: She had secured a Bible from a Huguenot pastor which she wanted him to read.) As she now stood in front of me, she meant to apologize...But I was no longer listening: "A Bible, you say? Where is it? Show me. I have never seen one before!" She complied. I literally grabbed the book and rushed to my study with it.

I opened it and "chanced" on the Beatitudes! I read, and read, and read—now aloud with an indescribable warmth surging within... I could not find words to express my awe and wonder. And all of a sudden, the realization dawned upon me: This was "the book that would understand me."

I needed it so much that I had attempted to write my own—in vain. I continued to read deep into the night, mostly from the Gospels. And lo and behold, as I looked through them, the One of whom they spoke, the One who spoke and acted in them, became alive to me.

The circumstances amid which the book had found me made it clear that while it seemed absurd to speak of a book understanding a man, this could be said of the Bible because its pages were animated by the presence of the living God. To this God I prayed that night, and the God who answered was the same God of whom it was spoken in the Book.

I still proceed on the theme of "the book that understands me."...My devotional life springs from my conversations with Holy Writ. Whenever I am confronted with difficulties, with a puzzling situation, or with a call on which more light is needed, I turn to a set of similar circumstances as presented in Scripture.

Or it may be that as I read the Bible, as a normal, daily practice, the passage "jumps at me" and lights up the way I must go.

Whatever the case may be, I pray over the page, waiting upon Him who speaks through it in a joyful eagerness to do His will. The margins of my Bible are marked with dates, with brief reminders of times when such a passage "spoke" to me and directed me.[5]

—Emile Cailliet

God's Word: Eternal

It was a beautiful spring day, May 21, a few years ago when I met my friend Bob Reinmiller at the Omaha, Nebraska airport. Bob was President of the Gospel Missionary Union with headquarters in Kansas City. We served together as Directors of an evangelical organization. After a good Board meeting we took Bob to the airport and said good-bye.

Five days later I wrote Bob a letter. In part it said, "Wish we could have had a lot more time together. It would be so nice to go fishing together or something relaxing like that."

Little did I know that Bob Reinmiller had already been in eternity two days when I wrote that letter. It will not be my privilege to have more time in this life with Bob Reinmiller—not for fishing or anything else.

Why do we not look forward more readily into that eternity toward which we all move? The Bible has that power.

"Heaven and earth will disappear—said Jesus—but my words will remain forever" (Mt. 24:35 nlt). A bold claim. How many men in the world's history have ever made such a claim? Few could stand with Jesus in such an affirmation. Fewer still, if any, would be believed.

"God has made everything beautiful for its own time. He has planted eternity in the human heart..."(Eccl. 3:11 nlt). "For what will it profit a man if he gains the whole world, and loses his own soul" (Mk. 8:36).

Dr. Donald Grey Barnhouse was a giant for God, one of the world's greatest Bible teachers of this century. He studied God's Word from 1913 to 1915 at the Bible Institute of Los Angeles. During that time he had a turning point in his attitude toward the Bible. Here is the anecdote as I came across it:

Barnhouse met Tom Haney, a man twice his age, who was State Secretary of Christian Endeavor. In Haney, Barnhouse found his guiding star.

They were on a train to a Christian Endeavor rally. Haney was reading his Bible, Barnhouse, a newspaper. Barnhouse finally dropped his newspaper, looked over at Haney and said, "Tom, I wish I knew my Bible like you know yours."

Barnhouse said later, "Without looking up, Tom said something I shall never forget as long as I live. He said, 'You'll never learn it reading the newspaper,' and back he went to his reading."

Said Barnhouse, "I can still see myself putting my newspaper down, leaning over, opening my briefcase, taking out my Bible and opening it. From that moment I made the utmost decision that nothing, nothing would ever stand between me and the Word of God.

"This was first and final."[6]

What Barnhouse called his "utmost decision" guided and tempered his life from that point on. It influenced his decisions and impacted his use of time.

How can the influence of the Bible be explained? Whence came the power of its words? Why is it so different from all other books?

No book ever written could properly be compared with the Bible. No one ever handled eternal themes so appropriately as Jesus. No biography ever recorded a life so perfect. No library could house the record of the lives He redeemed. No power to rebuild broken lives could match His own.

Have you ever made a pro-Bible choice? Decide now to read the Bible ambitiously every day. Feed you spirit more than you feed your body. God will transform you.

Forever is Real

Over the triple doorway of the Cathedral of Milan, there are three inscriptions spanning the splendid arches. A beautiful wreath of roses is carved over one of the arches, and underneath it are the words, "All that pleases is but for a moment."

Over a second arch is chiseled a cross, accompanied by the statement, "All that troubles is but for a moment."

But over the central entrance to the main portal one reads, "That only is important which is eternal."

Jesus taught His disciples, "Do not fear those who kill the body but cannot kill the soul. But rather fear him who is able to destroy both soul and body in hell" (Mt. 10:28). Death to the believer is merely an incident.

Again Jesus said to His followers, "Do not fear any of those things which you are about to suffer. Indeed the devil is about to throw some of you into prison...Be faithful until death, and I will give you the crown of life" (Rev. 2:10).

We live in an era of instant gratification. Jesus did not agree with "I want it now," especially as to rewards for right choices

When invited to a feast He said to his host, "When you put on a luncheon or a dinner, don't invite your friends, brothers, relatives, and rich neighbors. For they will repay you by inviting you back. Instead, invite the poor, the crippled, the lame, and the blind. Then at the resurrection of the godly, God will reward you for inviting those who could not repay you" (Lk. 14:12- nlt).

Jesus taught that we must wait for our reward. The Apostle Paul agreed. To his critics Paul replied, "What about me! Have I been faithful? Well, it matters very little what you or anyone else thinks. I don't even trust my own judgment on this point. My conscience is clear, but that isn't what matters. It is the Lord himself who will examine me and decide" (1 Co. 4:3- nlt).

A missionary in China was held up by bandits in a lonely place. They threatened to shoot him. The missionary looked the robber chief straight in the eyes and said without a tremor, "You shoot and I go straight to heaven." The bandit lost his courage when confronted by a man who was not afraid to die.

Evangelical pastor, John MacArthur, gives the following witness:

Nothing this world has to offer is more precious than God's Word. I have a friend who seeks rare Bibles. He owns a wonderful collection, with one Bible dating back to the fourth century.

But my favorite is a Bible from sixteenth-century England, one of the earliest printed copies of God's Word. The top third of this Bible is covered with the blood of its original owner. My friend let me hold it in my hands, and tears came to my eyes as I leafed through it.

How did blood get on the pages of that Bible? When Bloody Mary ruled England, she terrorized Protestants, murdering as many as she could. The soldiers would spill the person's blood, then take his Bible and dip it deep into the blood.

A few of those Bibles have been preserved and are known as Martyrs' Bibles. Scientists have tested the paper and confirmed that the dark stains on every page of my friend's Bible are human blood.

I examined that Bible carefully, page by page. I could see where it was well worn from being studied. There are water stains, as if from tears, and places where a thumb had frayed favorite pages. This was someone's most valuable possession, and his or her blood is there to prove it.

In sad contrast, however, contemporary Christians tend to take their Bibles for granted, forgetting that many have given their very lives just to own one copy.[7]

We believers in western nations are victims of our culture. We treat the Bible like any other commodity. A good book, we say, if cheap enough to be bought as we would buy any book. But we have forgotten that the Bible is unique. How desolate our destiny would be without it. Only the Bible brings us hope.

Weigh Jesus' words, "Heaven and earth will disappear, but my words will remain forever"(Mt. 24:35 nlt). Also, "Much is required from those to whom much is given, and much more is required from those to whom much more is given" (Lk. 12:4:4 nlt).

Jesus' Duel with Satan

Jesus' use of God's Word in his combat with Satan is amazing. He quoted Moses' words written 1400 years earlier. What an example for us. This was no chance encounter. It was basic in God's plan. "Jesus was led by the Spirit into the wilderness to be tempted by the devil. And when he had fasted forty days and forty nights, afterward he was hungry" (Mt. 4:1-).

Satan took advantage of His hunger saying, "If You are the Son of God, command that these stones become bread." Jesus quoted in reply, **"It is written, 'Man shall not live by bread alone, but by every word that comes from the mouth of God'"** (Mt. 4:4).

A blunt answer, but true. Physical food can feed the body, nothing more. Only God's Word can feed our spirit. **"People need more than bread (i.e. food) for their life; real life comes by feeding on every word of the Lord"** (Deut. 8:3 nlt).

The devil then set Him on the pinnacle of the temple and said, "If You are the Son of God, throw Yourself down, For it is written, 'He shall give His angels charge over you…lest You dash Your foot against a stone.'" Jesus' answered, **"It is written again, 'You shall not tempt the Lord your God'"**(Mt. 4:7).

The third temptation offered rulership as a reward for worshiping the devil. Again, the Bible answer, **"Away with you, Satan, for it is written, 'You shall worship the Lord your God and Him only you shall serve'"** (Mt. 4:10).

In this duel, Jesus used the same resource He has given us, God's Word. Otherwise His victory would have had little value to His followers.

Only constant review of Scripture could have given Jesus His ability to quote it. What an example for us! The goal is long-term. Will you pay the price? God asks His sheep to read and remember His Word daily, ambitiously, persistently. This is His way for His followers to live victoriously..

Jesus' example will do us no good unless we follow it. The phrase, "it is written" referred to the Old Testament. Moses had said, "Yes, he (God) humbled you by letting you go hungry and then feeding you with manna, a food previously unknown to you and your ancestors. He did it to teach you that people need more than bread for their life; real life comes by feeding on every word of the Lord" (Deut.8:3-). Hiding God's Word in the heart is the way to grow spiritually and to fight unbelief.

A critic of Moody, the statesman-evangelist, said he went to hear him with the confidence that he could show Moody to be a fraud. The reality surprised him. He said Moody seemed to hide behind the Bible, quoting text after text, until the man fell under deep conviction without finding the flaws in Moody he expected to criticize.

How many believers do you know who are able to quote a text of Scripture from memory in answer to an unwise proposal, argument or evident untruth? The example of Jesus must be our model.

To now you have read this book without much effort. But here you enter a different phase. Now comes work for you. The article "People and Ships" on page 38 pictures the bulk of humanity. I hope you belong to the Master's minority.

Do you resonate to the words "memorize and read the Bible in order to obey God?" That is the heart of the matter. Some people do what they ought, others do not. Which response is yours? I beg you to be "a doer of the word, and not a hearer only, deceiving yourself" (Jas.1:22).

If you accept the challenge the future belongs to you. As you obey God, Jesus will become more vital in your life. You will enjoy sweeter, more satisfying fellowship with Him. You will experience the "abundant life" our Lord promised in John 10:10.

As you agree more fully with Him, you will become more like Him. One day you will be surprised to hear yourself say, "In Your presence is fullness of joy; at Your right hand are pleasures forevermore" (Psa.16:11).

Alex Gosner

This is the amazing story of Alex Gosner. I was in a position to observe his conduct every working day. The man arrived at our Clinic in an extremely obnoxious and altered frame of mind. So true was this that none of the other patients, and not even our staff members, wanted to have any dealings with him. He was so rude and aggressive that everyone avoided him.

One day during a hard rain storm he asked me for boots and a raincoat to go out walking. He did not mind if it rained or stormed. He would go for his walks at all hours of the day, over the hills and through the valleys, but always returning in an almost violent mood, speaking harshly to those who chanced to cross his path.

One day a startling and unusual thing happened. I chanced to meet Mr. Gosner in the reception hall. Pointing his finger threateningly at me he said, "I need to speak to you." Let me assure you I was scared. I chose a place where everyone could see us, sat down, and asked him to do likewise.

He remained standing, however, and said, "I cannot sit down without having first expressed to you my appreciation and gratitude for the marvelous idea you had of placing a Bible in each room. My thanks go to your husband first, though I know he has passed away, but also to you." Then he sat down and continued.

"You have seen the way I acted during these past days. I simply had no peace within myself. My conscience accused me day and night of all the wicked things I have done throughout my life. I was in torment. While in this state, I took the Bible in my hands and began reading it.

"In reading this book a most marvelous thing has happened. Jesus is the Messiah and he is now my Savior. He died for my sins and I am free from the burden of guilt which I always carried within me. Also, I now feel a wonderful sense of joy and peace."

Well, we sat together for a long time talking about his

experience. I was still concerned, however, to make sure that he truly understood the message of the Gospel. Therefore I spoke to one of our believing doctors whose wife was also providentially present at the Clinic.

They then continued to talk with Mr. Gosner for another hour or so. They too were convinced that he had come to know Christ as his Savior and Lord. This became even more evident in the days that followed.

Six months later I received a letter from Mr. Gosner which transmitted his overflowing joy and peace. He told me he had already been baptized and was enjoying fellowship with all the believers in the church where he was worshiping.

But he also spoke of his deep sorrow because all his family were bitterly opposed to his decision.

Since no news came after that letter, I wrote him to inquire what church he was attending. My purpose was to put him in touch with other converted Jews, but I never received an answer. It is possible that the family intercepted the letter.

Even now I continue to pray for Alex Gosner and his family. Thus ends my account of the fascinating experience of the unusual visitor to our Sanatorio Diquecito.

The question remains, of course, as to how such a dramatic change of conduct can be explained? From one day to another the man's character changed drastically. What book do you know that could account for such a sudden, wonderful improvement in the man's whole outlook on life?

I know one Book, and only one, that has such power. It is the Bible. I bear witness to its power."[8]

—Irma Busse-Grawitz

Memorize To Obey

Are You Serious with God?

Card-carrying believers are needed, using Bible cards in spare moments to fill our lives with God's Word. Bible content should be a basic part of our talk. C. H. Spurgeon said, "What is in the well of your heart will come up in the bucket of your speech."

To quote God's Word correctly is not child's play. It is not an accident or a gift. Nor is it for Sunday School performances to make parents proud. Adults who neglect the Bible "rub out with their elbow what they write with their hand." Many damn the Bible with faint praise. Often excuses are made in an effort to hide indifference to God's Word.

What does quoting God's Word show? That you respect the Bible. It has been called "humanity's greatest asset." Yet believers are rare who can quote a dozen Bible verses. Fewer still know where even the best known texts are found.

When comments are made about my quoting Bible texts, one reply is, "It's a choice." In 1935 my failure started me memorizing texts. Over time, blessing has increased enormously. It can do the same for you.

This book can help you start today! Anyone who takes God seriously, can learn Bible verses and references. The decision is yours. I beg you, choose God's way.

Reflect carefully on the enormous consequences of choosing right. How willing are you to embrace a systematic plan to fill your life with God's Word? It's a decision God will honor.

Think, "How would God feel if I were to make that decision?" He is the one you should aim to please. Jesus set the standard, saying, "He who sent Me is with Me. The Father has not left Me alone, for I always do those things that please Him" (Jn. 8:29).

Why not make the decision to hide God's Word in your heart by following the plan recommended in these pages?

People and Ships

What are you looking for? The question is vital. "The Bible has enough light for those who desire to see—said Pascal—and enough darkness for those who only desire to hide from the truth."

The Bible will give you the answers you deserve. It will give you as much as you look for. Look for God, you will find Him; look for less, you will get that.

Truth before you offers you success. The promise is God's. Jesus said, "I did not come to call the righteous, but sinners..." (Mt. 9:13). Which are you? Do you agree with God by admitting. "I am a lost sinner? Or do you say with humble gratitude, "I am a sinner saved by grace?" To agree with Jesus is vital to His hearing your prayer. He came seek and to save sinners.

Thomas Carlyle said the book of Job was "one of the grandest things ever written." Job said, "Man is born to trouble as the sparks fly upward" (Job 5:7). Every generation since Job's day have proved his word true! Everyone should prepare for storms, for they will come. How about you? Will a crisis crowd you to Christ and the Bible too late?

People are like a ship going to sea. A few days out from port a storm strikes. The ship springs leaks, water pours in. The power fails, the holds are flooded. The captain and crew are helpless.

Now, what's the real problem? The ship isn't seaworthy and never was. But what a terrible time to find it out! So the doomed ship sinks lower and lower under the fury of the storm, At last comes the final plunge. All aboard go to a watery grave.

What would common sense have counseled? The answer is plain. The time to make the ship tight was in the dry dock early on.

Yet that ship pictures most people . They brush past the Bible to launch out on life's broad sea. For a time all is well. Then the storm strikes. Disaster!

It's too late now to start searching the Bible. Ahead? All dark. The Bible says, "It is appointed for people to die once, but after this the judgment" (Heb. 9:27). Wisdom says, read, memorize, meditate the Bible every day. The message, Life-Success Promise, page 39, is one of the most important you will ever consider.

Life-Success Promise

God made a huge promise to Joshua who faced a giant task. Moses was dead; Joshua was to take his place. God said, **"This Book of the Law shall not depart from your mouth, but you shall meditate in it day and night, that you may observe to do according to all that is written in it. For then you will make your way prosperous, and then you will have good success"** (Jos. 1:8).

God's condition was that Joshua would obey his Word. In order to do that Joshua had to read, memorize and meditate Scripture. God promised: "You will be prosperous and successful." In what? In everything you do!

In Psalm 1 God makes the same promise to everyone, including you, as He made to Joshua. He tells what you can do to enjoy His guarantee of success. God's condition? Obey His Word. God's promise? "Whatever you do will prosper."

The profile of the person God will bless, indeed, must bless, follows: **"His delight is in the law of the Lord, and in His law he meditates day and night. He shall be like a tree planted by the rivers of water that brings forth its fruit in its season, whose leaf also shall not wither; and whatever he does shall prosper"** (Psa. 1:2-).

For a third time God repeats His promise. **"The fear of the Lord is clean, enduring forever; the judgments of the Lord are true and righteous altogether. More to be desired are they than gold, yea, than much fine gold; sweeter also than honey and the honeycomb. Moreover by them Your servant is warned, and in keeping them there is great reward"** (Psa. 19:9-). The laws of God are more precious than gold, sweeter than honey, and "in keeping them there is great reward." Amazing! God's three-fold promise! This is one of the most astounding offers in God's Word. God guarantees to prosper, without limits, anyone who treats God's Word as He asks. That means to read and memorize the Bible in order to obey God as a permanent way of life.

God expresses the same purpose when he says in Luke's gospel, "Man shall not live by bread alone, but by every word of God" (Lk. 4:4). This book will guide you as you commit to do it.

Byron, a witness

Dr. Ralph L. Byron, was chief surgeon for more than two decades at City of Hope, the famous medical center.

Byron admits, "I rationalized, I'm too busy to do much about Christian interests, about the things of God. But one day, right in the midst of such reasoning God had a message for me, a verse that spoke to the depths in me: **'And I sought for a man among them that should make up the hedge, and stand in the gap before me... but I found none'** (Ez. 22:30).

"That Bible verse was to have a profound, lifelong impact on me. I never got away from it."

He was once asked, "What makes believers weak in their faith?" He answered, "I suspect the greatest weakness is that most believers do not memorize the Word. I used the Word of God daily at the City of Hope. I always quoted Scripture without editorial comment.

"One day, on my daily rounds, I came to a beautiful 27-year-old girl dying of breast cancer. I began to comfort her by reciting the Word of God. She told me as I finished that while I was reciting the Word she received Christ. Later, her father confirmed her faith by telling me that during the Scripture quotation she lost all fear.

"Our assignment from God is to store His Word away. The Word is now open and free to us. Soon it may be taken away."

When Dr. Byron began memorizing, he said, "I tried one verse and then another, only to discover that I couldn't remember the first one. It must have sounded like, 'I told you so,' when I complained to God I couldn't memorize. His response was, 'Review them some more.' So, it took a conscious effort on my part to memorize Scripture. But what dividends since I began "hiding God's Word in my heart."[9]

Byron tested God's offer and found Him to be worthy of total trust. Someone has said, "Imitation is the tribute that mediocrity pays to genius." Why not pay that tribute by doing what Byron did?

God makes the same incredible offer to you. Make memorizing God's Word a permanent good work honoring Jesus Christ.

My Poverty God's Plan

My conversion to Christ took place October 21, 1934, while a pre-med student at the University of Nebraska. The next summer I went to Moody Bible Institute in Chicago for a summer course. Early on I was asked to go with a student group to hold a street meeting.

In a station wagon we drove south on Michigan. On location we set up an organ and folding platform as our leader outlined the plan. We would begin with a few choruses and testimonies. Then, when he started the message, each of us would talk with someone about the Lord. I was scared stiff. A black man was seated in a doorway nearby. The message began, I moved toward him cautiously, and finally said, "Good afternoon."

He grunted a response.

"Are you a Christian?" I asked timidly.

"No," he almost roared.

Weak, but pressing on, I said, "Would you like to be?"

"Yes," he bellowed.

That word left me totally unstrung. Certain of a "No" answer, my preparation had been only for that. Had he said no, I had two or three weak arguments in mind. They probably would not have converted a mosquito, but they were all I had.

But the man had said, "Yes." What to do? I suddenly remembered the Bible under my arm. I opened it and began a rapid study, beginning at Genesis. I paged through the whole Bible to Revelation.

But something awful had happened. I could not find any verse I had ever seen before. Desperate, I started a Bible study from back to front like our Oriental friends do. But that was no better. All the time—it seemed forever—the man's eyes were boring into my face.

At last I said lamely, "God bless you," turned and walked away. Minutes later I climbed into the van with the others and we left. Slumped in my seat, utterly dejected, I said nothing during the trip back.

Once there, I climbed three flights of stairs to my room, locked the door behind me, threw myself across the bed and cried like a baby. I said to God, "What a fool I am. For the first time in my life I have been face to face with a man who said he wanted to become a

Christian and I didn't even know one Bible verse to give him."

Then and there I promised God I would never go out to witness without having two or three Bible texts so well-learned that no stage-fright could make me forget them.

You see, I had not read the Apostle Peter's advice, "If you are asked about your Christian hope, always be ready to explain it" (1 Pet. 3:15). Every believer should know a few Bible verses that tell plainly how a person can be saved. How can you prepare best? With or without a plan?

Soon after, a student I had recently met walked past me in the hall holding some cards in one hand and muttering under his breath. I said, "What are you doing, Phil?"

"Reviewing Bible verses," he said. Soon I was memorizing Bible texts from cards. That became the most significant activity of my life. I was like a miner who early in life stumbles onto an incredible vein of pure gold.

Years later I discovered another mother lode of gold in the rewards of daily Bible reading. The impact on my spiritual life was incredible. Words can't describe it!

The spirit must be fed more often than the body. Otherwise, the earthly culture and surroundings into which we were born overpower our new life in Christ. We wrongly expect two or three hours per week of exposure to the Bible to mold our character more than the scores of hours we spend in a worldly environment.

The logic is simple. We must reverse that situation. Compare feeding your body with feeding your spirit. The body is for this life only. It is temporary and will soon return to dust. The spirit is eternal and after death, which Jesus said we are not to fear, our spirit will live forever with the Lord.

The plan is obvious. We must repent of our inconsistency and do daily Bible reading worthy of our repentance. Begin at once to correct the imbalance by investing more time and effort in feeding your spirit than in feeding your body. This is not a short sprint, but a life-long marathon. Ask God's help, then start to rebuild your habits..

One plan is to start the day reading the Bible (p. 88) and praying (p.59). At noon review learned texts (p.43 & 68) and work on newest one. At night read God's Word and meditate it. Cry to God for help for so much depends on you. God is faithful.

Choose!

This may be a continental divide for you. To vary by a few inches where a drop of rain falls in the Rocky Mountains may cause it to flow west to the Pacific or southeast to the Gulf of Mexico. A vast difference in destinations! Bible memory work means nothing to most believers. Seen in the light of God's purpose for His people, it is weighty and worthwhile.

To now you have read this book without much effort. Here you enter a different phase. Now comes work. The article "People and Ships," page 38, pictures the bulk of humanity. I hope you belong to the Master's minority.

Will you hide God's Word in your heart, obedient to what He wants you to do? To delay decision says no. Yes means a new work of God in you.The next paragraph can be your start in a discipline filled with joy. Though I do not know you, I pray now that you will embrace God's best for you.

1. Receive Christ

Men asked, "What shall we do, that we may work the works of God?" Jesus answered, "This is the work of God, that you believe in Him whom He sent" (Jn. 6:29-). To believe in Christ is to receive Christ.

The Bible says, **"As many as received Him, to them He gave the right to become children of God, to those who believe in His name" (Jn. 1:12).** Ask yourself, "Have I received Christ?" If unsure you have received Him, do it now!

Life's greatest question concerns Christ. Do you know Him? He is the key to everything. Have you found Him? Dare you stand up for Him? Live for Him?

Jesus Christ says, **"Whoever confesses Me before men, him will I also confess before My Father who is in heaven. But whoever denies Me before men, him will I also deny before My Father who is in heaven" (Mt. 10:32–).**

Do not confuse any religious practice with the reality of receiving Christ. To have Him is much more than praying for health, a job, or for safety on a trip. Faith that saves is to believe Christ died for your sins and rose from the dead to give you eternal life, and that He is your Savior and Lord forever.

The Apostle Paul says **"That if you confess with your mouth the Lord Jesus and believe in your heart that God has raised Him from the dead, you will be saved"** (Rom. 10:9).

Do not treat this truth lightly. Christ is the only door to life eternal. If you have not done so, invite Him into your heart. See Revelation 3:20. God has told you the way to be saved. There is no other.

Guidelines:

1. Pause, ask God's help, then start. Texts to memorize are in bold type. Copy on a blank card the Theme Card title, "Receive Christ," and the references (See page 45). Write them as shown so your thumb will cover the references as you review, forcing you to think and visualize them.

2. Choose your Bible version with care. My choice is the New King James, because it is reliable and easier to memorize than most. Texts in this book are from the nkj unless otherwise noted. Overlearn John 1:12. before starting on Matthew 10:32– (See page 46).

3. When more than one Bible verse is quoted, such as Mt.10:32–33, only the first is noted with a dash: (Mt. 10:32–). Why? Text is shorter, thus easier to memorize. See Contents, page 3, for full quotation..

4. Don't be surprised if the first texts are tough to learn. To memorize John 1:12 may take several days. But keep at it; it will get easier. Be hard on yourself. Triumph is worth the effort. Be hungry for God's highest and best.

Billy Graham

The greatest regret I have tonight is that I didn't **memorize** more Scripture when my mind was keen and able to memorize. As you get older it gets more difficult.

—Billy Graham on an "Hour of Decision" telecast.

Theme Card and Text Card

Receive Christ

First
Theme
Card

Jn. 1:12
Mat. 10:32
Ro. 10:9

Cover references with
thumb when reviewing

*But as many as received
him, to them gave he power
to become the children of
God, even to them that believe
on his name.*

Front of
first text
card

Jn. 1:12

Back of
first text
card

Cards: are 9.5 cms. (3 3/4 inches) long, by 5.7 cms.
(2 1/4 inches wide).

Theme and Its Text Cards

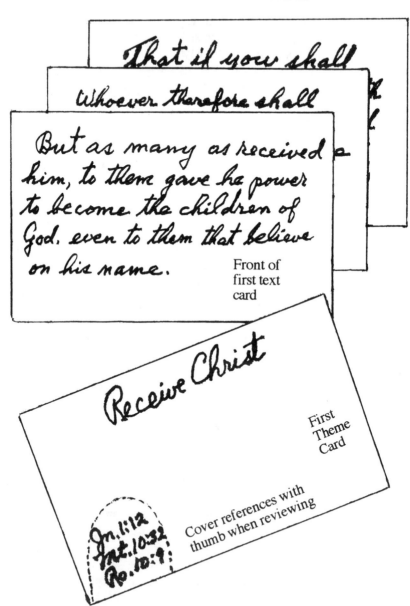

That if you shall

Whoever therefore shall

But as many as received him, to them gave he power to become the children of God, even to them that believe on his name.

Front of first text card

Receive Christ

First Theme Card

Jn. 1:12
Mt. 10:32
Ro. 10:9

Cover references with thumb when reviewing

2. Believe God

Jesus Christ wants you to win. He says, "To him who overcomes, I will give the right to sit with Me on My throne, just as I overcame and sat down with My Father on His throne" (Rev. 3:21).

Triumph is the believer's birthright. You say, "Then why am I defeated?" Are you practicing God's plan for victory? Use it well.

God wants you to be a winner. The texts that follow show you how. Note what God told Joshua when he faced an awesome task. Moses had died and Joshua was expected to fill his shoes.

God told him, **"This Book of the Law shall not depart from your mouth, but you shall meditate in it day and night, that you may observe to do according to all that is written in it. For then you will make your way prosperous, and then you will have good success"** (Jos. 1:8).

Was the promise only to Joshua? No. We find it elsewhere in the Bible. For centuries the Psalms have been the hymnal of the Church. The first Psalm pictures the person God promises to bless with success. **"His delight is in the law of the Lord, and in His law he meditates day and night. He shall be like a tree planted by the rivers of water, that brings forth its fruit in its season, whose leaf also shall not wither; and whatever he does shall prosper"** (Psa. 1:2–). What a great truth! Indeed it is the foundation for triumphant living.

King David, the sweet singer of Israel, further reinforces this truth saying, **"The fear of the Lord is clean, enduring forever; the judgments of the Lord are true and righteous altogether. More to be desired are they than gold, yea, than much fine gold; sweeter also than honey and the honeycomb. Moreover by them Your servant is warned, and in keeping them there is great reward"** (Psa. 19:9–).

If the book stopped here, would you act on God's promise? Do it for your eternal good. Few promises in the Bible have such power to transform your life! The three texts quoted above are very important. Obey them and you will never be the same. Take God at His word. He waits for proof that you love and trust Him.

Guidelines:

5. Whatever time it takes, learn John 1:12 perfectly by reading it aloud and repeating it often; only then go to Matthew 10:32–. Master that, before starting Romans 10:9. Pay the price to get every word right. That is your short-term goal.

6. Research shows that a text read once is 66% lost in 24 hours and is almost forgotten in 30 days. A text spoken several times a day for 8 days is nearly memorized; after 30 days the memory holds 90 % of the text. To say verses aloud daily is essential. Please, take these Guidelines to heart.

7. Overlearn the "Receive Christ" texts before starting "Believe God," verses. When you can say the first three texts perfectly, write Theme 2 card and its three text cards using same format as for Theme 1. Remember, texts to memorize are in bold type.

8. Please understand that to memorize fast is not the main aim; what counts is accuracy. Learn each text word for word as found in the Bible. When you have mastered perfectly the first six texts, start Theme 3.

9. Your Daily Pack will hold all theme and text cards until you complete Theme 8. Write each card carefully. The plan without cards would be a car without wheels or a plane without wings. Treasure your cards. With proper care they will last many years.

To Master a Tough Text

Read or say it 25 times the 1st day, always give reference 1st & last; 2nd day do drill 20 times, reference 1st & last; 3rd day 15 times; 4th day 10 times; 5th day 5 times. Then once a day for 7 weeks. **Whenever, in the process, you feel sure you have learned the text, put the card back in its proper place in the review sequence.**

3. Obey God

God commands us to obey Him. Obedience is non-negotiable. Adam and Eve got our race into big trouble when they disobeyed God. We all tend to think we are wiser than God. Though we might not say it openly, when temptation comes, at times we disobey God by decisions that show we do indeed think we are wiser than He is.

God says, **"And these words which I command you today shall be in your heart. You shall teach them diligently to your children, and shall talk of them when you sit in your house, when you walk by the way, when you lie down, and when you rise up" (Deut. 6:6–).** What a practical plan for memorizing God's Word. Right?

"My son, keep my words, treasure my commands within you. Keep my commands and live, and my law as the apple of your eye. Bind them on your fingers; write them on the tablet of your heart" (Prov. 7:1–).

God's order that we obey him spans the whole Bible. Its importance to the early church is revealed by Peter's statement, **"And we are His witnesses to these things, and so also is the Holy Spirit whom God has given to those who obey Him" (Acts 5:32).**

The Bible says obedience is better than any offering you might give to God (1 Sam. 15:22). Determine to do what He asks in every area of life. That way you will not fall prey to the world's evil.

Guidelines:

10. Keep Daily Pack with you **always.** It is essential, like purse or billfold. Why? So you can review each text at least once a day, more often if you can! Your aim should be to have every text in your arsenal ready on your lips.

11. Paul says, "Redeem the time." How? Review texts in minutes you would otherwise lose. This habit costs effort to develop. But work at it. It is very vital. "Set your mind on things above, not on things on the earth" (Col.3:2).

Charles Swindoll on Memorizing Scripture

I know of no other single practice in the Christian life more rewarding, practically speaking, than memorizing Scripture.

That's right. No other single discipline is more useful and rewarding than this. No other single exercise pays greater spiritual dividends!

Your prayer life will be strengthened. Your witnessing will be sharper and much more effective. Your counseling will be in demand. Your attitudes and outlook will begin to change. Your mind will become alert and observant. Your confidence and assurance will be enhanced. Your faith will be solidified.

God's word is filled with exhortations to implant His truth in our hearts. David says that a young man can keep his life pure by treasuring God's Word in his heart (Psalm 37:31; 119:9-11). Solomon refers to this in Proverbs 4:4:

...Let your heart hold fast my words;
   keep my commandments and live.

The words "hold fast" come from a single Hebrew term, meaning "to grasp, seize, lay hold of." Scripture memory gives you a firm grasp of the Word—and allows the Word to get a firm grasp of *you*! Solomon also mentions writing the Word "on the tablet of your heart" (Proverbs 7:3) and having Scriptures kept within you so "they may be ready on your lips" (Proverbs 22:18).

Now, I know you've been challenged to do this before. But is it happening?[10]

4. Eat Bible.

Jesus Christ said, "I tell you the truth, unless you eat the flesh of the Son of Man and drink His blood, you have no life in you. Whoever eats My flesh and drinks My blood has eternal life." (Jn. 6:53–).

For Christ to save you, you must receive Him spiritually as you assimilate food physically. Why do so few believers hunger for God's Word? Such apathy is sad. A true appetite for the Bible, and a heart to obey God, is His formula for spiritual health.

Jeremiah said, **"Your words were found, and I ate them, and Your word was to me the joy and rejoicing of my heart; for I am called by Your name, O Lord God of hosts" (Jer. 15:16).**

And Jesus said, **"It is written, 'Man shall not live by bread alone, but by every word that proceeds from the mouth of God'" (Mt. 4:4).** We must feed on the whole Bible.

The Apostle Peter reinforced that fact with the words, **"As newborn babies, desire the pure milk of the word, so that you may grow thereby, if indeed you have tasted that the Lord is gracious" (1 Pet. 2:2–).**

Guidelines:

12. Use this test. Practice the text alone. Next, say it to your mother, sister, brother, aunt. Do that regularly before you quote it to an acquaintance. Don't fool yourself. Quoting texts to others is much harder than doing it alone.

13. It is a skill to quote texts meaningfully. You will be afraid, but God will help you. This is His plan. He promises results (Isa. 55:11). When sure of all prior portions, copy Theme 4 and its texts.

14. Always repeat the reference aloud before and after you say the text as an aid to memory. If you find it hard to remember the first words of a text, write the first three or four words several times. Do that every day until you master them.

Survival Secret

My grandmother has seen two world wars and a depression. She bore one daughter and one son. She buried the son. She lost one husband at 40, and another at 66. Yet through all the days of her life, one thing remained constant and essential, her habit of memorizing the Bible.

I recall glorious Sunday afternoons on the old porch swing telling grandmother verses I had memorized. One of the first verses I learned during World War 2 was Proverbs 3:3, "Let love and faithfulness never leave you, bind them around your neck, write them on the tablet of your heart." She was always reinforcing God's eternal commitment to us.

Grandmother had a verse of Scripture for every occasion. When my sister and I were quarreling she would quote from Psa.133, "How good and how pleasant it is for brothers to live together in unity." We would laugh because we were girls.

When we criticized others, out would pop Matthew 7:1, "Judge not, that you be not judged." When I doubted my salvation, grandmother would quote 1 John 5:12, "He who has the Son has life; he who does not have the Son of God does not have life." There was a verse for every situation in life from anger to zeal.

One of grandmother's biggest fears was that she would end up in a nursing home. Sadly, she has been in one now for almost three years. She turned 100 last May and is losing her sight and hearing. But grandmother was wise. In her later years she read and memorized the Bible more than ever before.

Little did she know how glad she would be for that self discipline. For now her greatest strength is her ability to recall hundreds of verses to get her through the long days. She is an inspiration to all who visit her. And we know that when we visit her we had better come prepared with some verses to share.[11]   —Rose Keilhacker

5. Serve Others

Perhaps no term describes the believer better than "serve" or "servant." How profound is Christ's word, **"You know that the rulers of the Gentiles lord it over them, and those who are great exercise authority over them. Yet it shall not be so among you; but whoever desires to become great among you, let him be your servant. And whoever desires to be first among you, let him be your slave—Just as the Son of Man did not come to be served, but to serve, and to give His life a ransom for many" (Mt. 20:25–).**

If ever a Bible portion seemed to probe the heart of our proud nature, the one just quoted does. Christ sheds further light on this high standard by a word picture in Luke 17. He concludes, **"So likewise you, when you have done all those things which you are commanded, say, 'We are unprofitable servants. We have done what was our duty to do'" (Lk. 17:10).**

More moving than words was the way Christ exemplified the principle of unselfish service. **"Now before the feast of the Passover, when Jesus knew that His hour had come that He should depart from this world to the Father, having loved His own who were in the world, He loved them to the end" (Jn. 13:1).**

He then took a towel, wrapped it about Himself, and washed His disciples' feet. Christ's actions, in that setting, made humble, selfless service the hallmark of His followers through all the ages.

Guidelines:

15. You will use or lose texts you have learned. Find a family member or friend willing to listen to God's Word. Start there. As you quote texts to others, your comfort zone will expand. Share because you care. Quoted texts have power to make people "wise unto salvation, through faith in Christ Jesus" (2 Tim. 3:15).

16. Learn each text 100% right. Be patient. Never move on from a text before mastering it, for that will slow you down eventually. To aid quick review, every text must be over learned. Rapid review saves you time. Prepare for it.

"Memorize and Meditate"

For most of my life I have had a serious problem with anger. It consumed me. I became so angry I threw things and did damage. It was dangerous to my husband and children.

Trying to tell myself not to get angry didn't help. Counseling did no good. One day the pastor exhorted us to obey God. He did biblical counseling. I finally sought his help.

During one of our sessions he suggested I read Norm Lewis' book, *Success God's Way*. After I read it I started memorizing verses from the Bible on anger.

In just a few days something wonderful happened. The Lord gave me an incredible peace that comes only from Him, and the raging inferno I had always felt inside me was gone. I was healed!

The Bible teaches that anger is a God-given emotion, but we are not to sin when angry. Eph. 4:26–27. So I study my Bible, memorize and meditate verses, and the more I do this the closer I get to being like Christ, Hallelujah.[12]

—Linda Perez

6. Make Disciples

Our attitude as Christ's followers is to serve, but our goal is to "make disciples." Those two words sum up the true believer's passion and purpose. They make total demands on his life.

After His resurrection Christ affirmed, **"All authority has been given to Me in heaven and on earth. Go therefore and make disciples of all the nations, baptizing them in the name of the Father and of the Son and of the Holy Spirit, teaching them to observe all things that I have commanded you; and lo, I am with you always, even to the end of the age" (Mt. 28:18-).**

One secret of disciple-making is example. The Apostle Paul said, **"The things which you learned and received and heard and saw in me, these do, and the God of peace will be with you" (Phil. 4:9).**

The disciple-maker must exemplify what he asks others to be and do. Paul showed that this was basic to God's plan to evangelize the world when he said, **"And the things that you have heard from me among many witnesses, commit these to faithful men who will be able to teach others also" (2 Ti. 2:2).**

Guidelines:

17. The best thing you ever did was to receive Christ as your Savior and Lord. Right? Therefore, the best thing you can do for anyone else is to lead him to Christ. Let that truth empower you to witness whenever the Holy Spirit prompts you to do so. And listen for His voice!

18. Let God's command to make disciples (Mt. 28:19-) cause you to be very vigilant about your own example. How potent the words, "Those things which you...saw in me, do, and the God of peace will be with you!"

19. Disciple-making means to share with a friend by example and word the blessing of biblical obedience. "Show and tell" is God's plan. Pray about inviting a friend to work through this book with you.

Jeremiah's Menu

"Jeremiah wrote, **"Your words were found, and I ate them, and Your word was to me the joy and rejoicing of my heart; for I am called by Your name, O Lord God of hosts"** (Jer. 15:16).

Suppose God were to tell you, "Feed on my Word as often as you eat? Would you understand and obey? But is God not saying that?

Which is more important, to feed your immortal spirit, or to feed your body, which will soon return to dust? Is God not saying, "Feed your spirit as often as you feed your body?" It's simple logic.

Honor this plea; follow God's reasoning. Read at the start of the day, carry memory cards for use at noon, and at night read seriously before you sleep. The plan is radical; over time it will produce powerful results.

Saturate heart and mind with God's Word by reading and memorizing the sacred text in order to obey God. It will change you from the inside out.

7. Know Christ

To merely nominal religious people Christ will one day say, "I never knew you. Depart from Me" (Mt. 7:21). Can you imagine more frightening words? Assurance of salvation is vital. The true believer presses on, seeking always to grow in the grace and knowledge of Christ.

How wonderful that our Lord excludes no one, believer or not, from His loving invitation, **"Come to Me, all you who labor and are heavy laden, and I will give you rest. Take My yoke upon you and learn from Me, for I am gentle and lowly in heart, and you will find rest for your souls. For My yoke is easy and My burden is light"** (Mt. 11:28–).

He himself said, **"And this is life eternal, that they may know You, the only true God, and Jesus Christ whom You have sent" (Jn. 17:3).**

Growth in the knowledge of Christ, however, must not stop. The Apostle Paul said, **"But any advantages I had I considered a loss for Christ. Yes, I think it is all a loss because it is so much better to know Christ Jesus, my Lord. For Him I have lost everything and consider it garbage in order to win Christ" (Phil. 3:8– Beck).**

Paul knew Christ, yet he said, "I want to know Him..." (Phil. 3:10). He longed to know Christ better.

You can only know God through His Son. Just before the wonderful invitation quoted above, Jesus said, "No one knows the Father except the Son and those to whom the Son chooses to reveal Him" (Mt.11:27). To receive Christ, and to know God through Him, is our priceless privilege.

Guidelines:

20. Start each day with God. Meet Him first and what follows will go better. Commit the day to His control. Read the Bible, pray, and hide the Word in your heart. "As for me, how good it is to be near God! I have made the Sovereign Lord my shelter, and I will tell everyone about the wonderful things you do" (Psa.73:28 nlt).

Why I Memorize
SCRIPTURE

1
To use against temptation.
2
To renew my mind.
3
To encourage others.
4
To remain alert in battle.
5
To be prepared for
unbelievers' questions.
6
To maintain an accurate
picture of God.
7
To recover fellowship with
Him after I sin.
8
To increase my faith.
9
To obtain power for obedience.
1 0
To gain insight and guidance.[17]
—by Chris West

8. Pray Always

Do not wait to understand prayer before you pray. Pray because Jesus prayed and taught believers to pray. Pray because the Bible is built on answered prayer. God promised Jeremiah, **"Call to Me, and I will answer you, and show you great and mighty things, which you do not know" (Jer. 33:3).**

Jesus taught the importance of prayer with words so simple a child can understand them. **"But you, when you pray, go into your room, and when you have shut your door, pray to your Father who is in the secret place; and your Father who sees in secret will reward you openly" (Mt. 6:6).**

The power of prayer is as great as the greatness of God. Jesus said, **"If you abide in Me, and My words abide in you, you will ask what you desire, and it shall be done for you" (Jn. 15:7).**

"Pray without ceasing" (1 Thess. 5:17) is God's word to you. Talk to to Him throughout the day. Practice His presence. David said, "I have set the Lord always before me; because He is at my right hand I shall not be moved" (Psa. 16:8). Dr. John R. Rice said, "Prayer is asking; answered prayer is receiving."

Charles Spurgeon painted a word picture, saying, "Prayer pulls the rope down below and the great bell rings above in the ears of God. Some scarcely stir the bell, for they pray so languidly; others give only an occasional jerk at the rope. But he who communicates with heaven is the man who grasps the rope boldly and pulls continuously with all his might."

Jesus taught that a childlike attitude in prayer is right. He said, "Ask and it shall be given to you; seek, and you will find; knock, and it will be opened to you. For everyone who asks receives, and he who seeks finds, and to him who knocks it will be opened" (Mt. 7:7-).

Guidelines:
21. Scripture in your heart will stagnate if not shared. You are blessed to be a blessing. David declared it was worth more than gold and was sweeter than honey. Carry and use your Daily Pack in order to keep texts ready on your lips. Often remind yourself, "I am not ashamed of the gospel of

Christ, for it is the power of God to salvation for everyone who believes" (Rom.1:16).

22. You are ready to add Theme 9. Right? Remove Theme 1, "Receive Christ", plus its text cards from Daily Pack; with them start Pack Two. Put a rubber band around them and keep them with your Bible. Copy Theme 9 with its text cards and add them to the front of your Daily Pack.

Effective Prayer

Effective prayer must be in the name of Jesus. For instance, my son can sign his name on my accounts because of his relationship to me. So it is with us and God. We must have a close relationship.

Jesus said, "If you abide in Me and my words abide in you, you will ask what you desire, and it shall be done for you" (Jn.15:7). We must be totally yielded to Him.

Some ask me what total commitment is. My answer is, if you come to the City of Hope with cancer we ask if you want us to operate. You then have a decision to make.

If you decide yes, you are 100% committed to us. Your life is totally in our hands. Jesus asks no less.[9]

—*Dr. Ralph Byron.*

9. Share Bible

The believer's best tool and weapon is God's Word. It has been true in every epoch. God said, **"So shall My word be that goes forth from My mouth; it shall not return to Me void, but it shall accomplish what I please, and it shall prosper in the thing for which I sent it"** (Isa. 55:11).

Jeremiah wrote, **"Is not My word like a fire?"** says the Lord, **"And like a hammer that breaks the rock in pieces?"** (Jer. 23:29)

The writer of Hebrews says, **"For the word of God is living and powerful, and sharper than any two-edged sword, piercing even to the division of soul and spirit, and of joints and marrow, and is a discerner of the thoughts and intents of the heart"** (Heb. 4:12).

Guidelines:

23. Stay on track. Many start, few stay the course. Carry Daily Pack with you always. Try review without removing cards from the case. As a theme comes to mind, can you recall its texts? Practice that way.

24. You have reached Theme 10, "Be Wise." Add this theme with its cards to your Daily Pack. Remove Theme 2 with its cards from Daily Pack and place them at the front of Pack Two, which till now has had only Theme 1. Find a container for Pack Two.

Bedrock

I have made a covenant with my God that He send me neither visions, dreams, nor even angels. I'm well satisfied with the gift of the Holy Scriptures, which give me abundant instruction and all that I need to now both for this life and for that which is to come.

I put Scriptures above all the sayings of the Fathers, Angeles, men and devils. Here I stand.

—Martin Luther

Shields and Swords

Every student will admit that, at least once, he or she memorized something—a math formula, maybe, or a sonnet or a date in history—just to repeat it for the test. Several weeks later, the fact gets forgotten.

For six college freshmen memorizing Bible verses together, life is the test, and they want to pass it every day. They know where to find answers, too—God's Word, which overflows with, practical, life-changing truths. But the students need to remember the answers they find in the Bible, and the test won't always be "open book."

"I am not just memorizing it," says one of the six. "I am committing to have this memorized always, to always know it."

Chris began building his "arsenal," as he calls it, during his junior university year in 1983. To the then-new believer, the Bible brimmed with undiscovered meaning and truth, and he wanted to know how to access the message between its covers.

"I developed an incredible love for the Scriptures," Chris says, "by observing seasoned believers around me who had a handle on the Word." He wanted that same kind of grip. "People would read references as if they were common knowledge and it would drive me crazy that I couldn't find them," Chris remembers. "I wanted to make sure that didn't happen for long."

Chris noticed a life change. By intentionally commiting all those verses to memory, he says they come up naturally in conversation, and more surprisingly, in his mind.

"It is just part of my thought life," says Chris. "That is why I memorize Scripture. I wanted those thoughts up there." He laughs out loud: "I've got enough problems with the other thoughts."

Chris works hard to remember. He now invests his energy to remember those weapons in the closet of his mind. And he helps others use Scripture memory to array an artillery against the demands of life and ministry.[17]

—*Erik Segalini*

10. Be Wise

King David said, **"I have more understanding than all my teachers, for Your testimonies are my meditation"** (Psa.119:99).

The words of King Solomon add their weight. **"Incline your ear and hear the words of the wise, and apply your heart to my knowledge; for it is a pleasant thing if you keep them within you; let them all be fixed upon your lips"** (Prov. 22:17–).

An aspect of wisdom we hear little about is brokenness—the only way to become like Christ. **"For thus says the High and Lofty One Who inhabits eternity, whose name is Holy: 'I dwell in the high and holy place, with him who has a contrite and humble spirit, to revive the spirit of the humble, and to revive the heart of the contrite ones'"** (Isa. 57:15).

Guidelines:
25. **FREE TO WITNESS:** One of the rewards of Scripture in your heart is added freedom to witness. Peter said, "Make Christ the holy Lord in your hearts. And always be ready to answer anyone who asks you to explain the hope you have, but be gentle and respectful" (1 Pet. 3:15 Beck). "He who wins souls is wise" (Prov. 11:30).
26. **DAILY PACK, WHY? You must review every day in order to retain texts and references long-term.** Carry the Daily Pack with you always. Review its 24 texts at least once a day. Many have done well in Bible memory until they began to forget memorized texts as fast as they learned new ones. Believe me, this plan offers a practical answer.

Body or Spirit?

"I have not departed from the commandment of His lips; I have treasured the words of His mouth more than my necessary food" (Job 23:12).

11. Evangelize World

God spoke to Israel, **"Indeed He said, 'It is too small a thing that You should be My Servant to raise up the tribes of Jacob, and to restore the preserved ones of Israel; I will also give You as a light to the Gentiles, that You should be My salvation to the ends of the earth'"** (Isa. 49:6).

Our Lord gave wisdom that every believer should live by and on which the very plan of his life should be built. He said, **"This gospel of the kingdom will be preached in all the world as a witness to all the nations, and then the end will come" (Mt. 24:14).**

And the task was given to all believers. By God's grace we have been made "a royal priesthood" (1 Pet. 2:9) to be the link between all humanity and God. He orders us, **"Go into all the world and preach the gospel to every creature. He who believes and is baptized will be saved; but he who does not believe will be condemned" (Mk. 16:15–).**

Guidelines:

27. **DAILY HOME REVIEW:** You fear it will take too much time. Not so! In one minute you can repeat aloud three average texts at a normal speech rate, giving reference first and last. Review ONLY two themes a day per pack beyond your Daily Pack. And since you have few cards in Pack Two, this will be easy if you start **now.** See WARNING below.

28. **HOME REVIEW, CRITICAL!** Imagine the day when you have memorized four packs. You will review two Themes in Pack Two (two minutes); two in Pack Three (two minutes); two in Pack Four (two minutes). Total: six minutes a day to keep ready 360 potent texts, God's answer to Satan's fiery darts.

     WARNING: DANGER TO YOUR SUCCESS! If now, when review is quick and easy, you excuse yourself from it, when you try later and find it hard, will you do it? Not likely.

God's Name, God's Word

"You have exalted above all things your name and your word."

Psalm 138:2 niv

12. Be Free

What can compare with the freedom God gives? The Psalmist wrote, **"He sent His word and healed them, and delivered them from their destructions"** (Psa. 107:20).

Jesus greatly enlarged the concept of freedom when he said, **"If you abide in My word, you are My disciples indeed. And you shall know the truth, and the truth shall make you free"** (Jn. 8:31–).

The final text in this group is from the last book of the Bible. Jesus said, **"I know your works. See, I have set before you an open door, and no man can shut it; for you have a little strength, have kept My word, and have not denied My name"** (Rev. 3:8).

Guidelines:
29. **DAILY PACK, A MUST!** Have your Daily Pack with you **always. Use any free bit of time to review its texts.** Unless you are very unusual, you will not at first be aware of those moments as they pass. Watch for them! Be alert! Develop the habit. Only this will you keep your heart and mind saturated with God's Word.

30. **PRO DAILY REVIEW: Give God's Word the priority it merits.** Give yourself to it every day. You will never again need to set dates and times for extra review (like at month's end). Minutes of time daily, memorizing in order to obey God, will keep you current and victorious, walking with Him.

31. **FOLLOW THIS PLAN to succeed** long-term memorizing and meditating the Bible. You will revisit less often those verses you have known longest, yet you will never abandon a text. That makes you a winner because you will retain all texts forever. Amen.

Review

Key to Long-Term Bible Memory

Dr. Ralph Byron knows review is essential to successful Bible memory work. He says:

"Early in my walk with Christ I was made aware of how little Bible I really knew. I was aboard ship during World War II when another doctor asked me to tell him about the Bible.

It became painfully obvious that I knew very little of the Bible. Here I had finished high school, college, medical school and had committed thousands of facts to memory, yet, knew none of God's Word. I had only played with the most important Book.

"Right then, the Lord said, 'Memorize.'"

Byron, "I can't."

God, "You can."

Byron, "I don't like to."

God, "You will."

Byron, "I will forget."

God, "Review, that's how you must learn."

God won the argument. Dr. Byron began methodically to memorize and review texts. He later said, "I used God's Word daily at the City of Hope."[9]

Priorities will make you or break you. What are your priorities?

Priorities are the things you do every day.

Themes: Your Choice

To see so many themes can be confusing. It's like, "How do you eat an elephant?" Answer, "One bite at a time." Pick themes that interest you. And keep going. Press on. Nothing can do as much to make you like our Lord as to swim in the ocean of His grace (see Rom. 8:29).

Live under God's guidance in the Bible. Hide His Word in your heart in order to obey Him and "whatever you do will prosper."

Abram's children
Rom. 4:11-12
Rom. 4:16
Rom. 9:8

Alcohol
Prov. 23:29-30
Prov. 23:31-32
Prov. 31:4

Alcohol 2
Isa. 5:11
Isa. 28:7
Hab. 2:15

Alcohol 3
Lk. 1:15
Rom. 14:21
Eph. 5:18

All, all, all
1 Ti. 2:1-2
1 Ti. 2:3-4
1 Ti. 2:5-6

All mine
Ezek. 24:28
Rom. 8:38-19
1 Cor. 3:21-23

Attitude
Rom. 4:20-21
Rom. 8:31-32
Heb. 12:1-2

Authority, Christ's
Jn. 10:35-36
Jn. 12:44-46
Jn. 12:47-50

Aware of God
Mt. 6:6
1 Cor. 4:4
Eph. 6:6

Balance
Lk. 2:52
Rom. 12:1-2
Tit. 2:11-12

Baptism
Mk. 16:16
Acts 2:38
Rom. 6:4

Baptism 2
1 Cor. 1:17
Col. 2:12
1 Pet. 3:21-22

Beautiful feet
Isa. 52:7
Rom. 10:15
Eph. 6:14-15

Believer
Mt. 10:32-33
Jn. 1:12
Rom. 10:9-10

Believer inherits
Rom. 8:16-17
Tit. 3:7
1 Pet. 1:3-4

Benedictions
Nu. 6:24-26
2 Cor. 13:14
Eph.3:20-21

Bened. 2
Heb. 13:20-21
2 Pet. 3:18
Jude 1:24-25

Bible assures
Jn. 5:24
Rom. 8:11
Jn. 5:11-12

Bible cleanses
Psa. 119:9-11
Jn. 15:3
Eph. 5:25-26

Bible essential
Jer. 5:4
Jer. 8:9
Jer. 9:12-13

Bible, faith
Rom. 4:20-21
Rom. 10:17
Heb. 4:2

Bible, hear
Prov. 8:34
Rom. 10:17
Rev. 2:7

Bible inspired
1 Ts. 2:13
2 Ti. 3:16
2 Pet. 1:21

Bible lasts
Psa.119:89-90
Psa. 119:152
Psa. 119:160

Bible, life
Jn. 6:63
Jn. 6:68
Phil. 2:16

Bible, light
Psa. 119:105
Prov. 6:23
2 Pet. 1:19

Bible, Meditate
Psa. 1:2-3
Psa.119:97
1 Ti. 4:1

Bible, Memorize
Deut. 6:6-7
Psa. 119:11
Prov. 7:1-3

Bible nourishes
Mt. 4:4
Acts 20:32
1 Pet. 2:2

Bible, Read
Dt. 17:18-19
1 Ti. 4:13
Rev. 1:3

Bible stands
Psa. 119:89
Mt. 24:35
Mt. 12:48

Bible, Study
Jn. 5:39
Acts 17:11
2 Ti.2:15

Bible, Teach
Ezra 7:10
Neh. 8:8
1 Ti. 4:13

Bible truth
Jn. 17:17
2 Ti.2:15
Jas. 1:18

Blind to truth
Isa. 5:20-21
Mt. 15:14
Mt. 23:24

Blind to truth 2
2 Co. 4:4
Eph. 4:18
2 Pet.1:9

Blood
Ex. 12:13
Lev. 17:11
Mt. 26:28

Blood 2
Heb. 9:11-12
Heb. 9:13-14
Heb. 9:22

Blood 3
1 Pet. 18:19
Rev. 1:5b-6
Rev. 12:11

Choose
Deut. 30:19
Josh. 24:15
1 K. 18:21

Choose 2
2 Ki. 17:41
Psa.109:17
Prov. 1:29-31

Choose 3
Mt. 12:30
Heb. 11:24-26
Rev. 22:11

Christ at hand
Psa. 16:8-9
Mt. 28:20
Acts 2:25-26

Christ, Authority
Jn. 10:35-36
Jn. 12:44-46
Jn. 12:47-50

Christ cares
Heb. 2:14
Heb. 2:18
Heb. 4:14-16

Christ died for me
Rom. 5:8
Gal. 2:20
Gal. 3:13

Christ died for me 2
1 Pet. 2:24
1 Pet. 3:18
1 Jn. 2:2

Christ, incomparable
Phil. 3:7-8
Col. 1:15-16
Rev. 19:11-13

Christ in me
Gal. 2:20
Eph. 3:17-19
Col. 1:27

Christ lives
Mk. 16:5-6
Lk. 24:30-31
Acts 10:40-41

Christ lives 2
1 Cor. 15:5-8
Rev. 1:17-18
Rev. 22:12-13

Christ, Prayer
Mt. 6:9-13
Mt. 7:11
Lk. 21:36

Christ preexisted
Jn. 8:58
Jn. 17:5
Phil. 2:5,6

Christ sinless
Mt. 27:4
Mt. 27:19
Mt. 27:54

Christ sinless 2
Lk. 23:41
Jn. 8:29
Jn. 8:46

Christ sinless 3
Jn. 14:30
Jn. 18:38
2 Cor. 5:21

Christ sinless 4
Heb. 4:15
1 Pet. 2:22
1 Jn.3:5

Christ, Supreme
Mt. 3:17
Mt. 17:5
Jn. 2:5

Christ, Supr. 2
Phil. 2:9-11
Col 1:15
Rev. 5:11-12

Church, Body
Rom. 12:4-5
1 Cor. 12:12
1 Cor. 12:27

Church, Body 2
Eph. 1:22-23
Eph. 5:29-30
Col. 2:19

Church discipline
Mt. 18:15-17
Acts 5:11
1 Ti. 5:19-20

Church purpose
Mt. 16:17-18
Eph. 1:4-5
1 Pet. 2:9-10

Closure
Jn. 4:34
Jn. 17:4
Jn. 19:30

Commit
Lk. 12:48
1 Ti. 1:18-19
2 Ti. 2:2

Complain
1 Cor. 10:10
Phil. 2:14
Jas. 5:9

Conflict
Eccl. 10:4
1 Ts. 5:12-13
Phile. 15

Conversion
Psa. 19:7
Psa. 51:12-13
Psa.119:59-60

Conversion 2
Mt. 4:19-20
Lk. 19:6-9
Gal. 1:23-24

Counsel
Prov. 18:13
Prov. 27:17
Prov. 28:23

Counsel 2
Mk. 6:30
I Cor. 14:3
1 Ts. 2:11

Criticism
Prov 3:11-12
Prov. 6:23
Prov. 15:31-32

Cross, death
2 Cor. 5:14-15
Gal. 2:20
Gal. 6:14-15

Cross, When?
(See Eternal Plan)

Daily focus
Prov. 4:20-21
Prov. 6:22
Prov. 7:1-3

Death, saints
Psa. 116:15
1 Ts. 4:14
Rev. 14:13

Death, Second
Rev. 20:6
Rev. 20:14-15
Rev. 21:8

Death, Spiritual
Gen. 2:17
Lk. 15:24
Jn. 5:25

Death, Spiritual 2
Jn. 10:10
1 Cor.15:22
Eph. 2:1

Devil
Isa. 14:12
Eze. 28:14-15
Acts 26:18

Devil 2
Eph. 6:11
2 Cor. 2:11
2 Cor. 11:14

Devil 3
1 Pet. 5:8
Rev. 12:9
Rev. 20:10

Disciple
Lk. 14:25-26
Lk. 14:27
Lk. 14:33

Discipline, Child
Prov. 13:24
Prov. 22:15
Prov. 23:13-14

Discipline, Child 2
Prov. 29:15
Prov. 29:17
Eph. 6:4

Do & teach
Mt. 5:19
Mt. 28:18-20
Mk. 6:30

Do & teach 2
Acts 1:1
Phil. 4:9
1 Ti. 4:15-16

Encourage
Psa. 20:4-5
Psa. 27:14
Psa. 34:18-19

Encourage 2
Prov. 12:25
Prov. 16:24
Prov. 18:21

Eternal plan
2 Ti. 1:9-10
1 Pet.1:20-21
Rev. 13:8

Eternity
Mk. 8:36-37
2 Cor. 4:18
1 Jn. 2:17

Evangelize
Jn.4:35-36
2 Ti. 4:2
1 Pet. 3:14-15

Example
Jud. 7:17
Mt. 4:19
1 Cor. 4:16

Example 2
1 Cor. 11:1
Gal. 4:12
Phil. 3:17

Example 3
Phil. 4:9
1 Ts. 1:6-7
2 Ts. 3:7

Faint not
Lk. 18:1
Gal.6:9
Heb. 12:3

Favoritism
Rom. 2:11
Rom. 3:22-23
Rom. 10:12-13

Fear God
Deut. 6:13
Jos. 24:14
1 Sam. 12:24

Fear God 2
Psa. 34:9
Psa. 61:5
Psa. 112:1

Fear not men
Prov. 29:25
Isa. 51:7-8
Isa. 51:12-13

First things
Mt. 6:33
Acts. 20:24
Phil. 3:7-8

Follow Christ
Lk. 9:23
1 Pet. 2:21
1 Jn. 2:6

Forgive all
Mt. 6:14-15
Mt. 18:21-22
Mt. 18:34-35

Forgive all 2
Mk. 11:25-26
Eph. 4:31-32
Col. 3:12-13

Fortitude
1 Co.16:13-14
Jas. 1:12
1 Pet. 1:6-7

Foundation
Mt. 7:24-25
1 Cor. 3:11
2 Ti. 2:19

Freedom
Jn. 8:31-32
Gal. 5:1
1 Pet. 2:16

Future, Focus
Phil. 2:16
1 Ts. 2:19-20
1 Jn. 2:28

Gifts, Spirit
Rom. 12:6
1 Cor. 12:8-10
1 Cor. 14:12

Gift to each
1 Cor. 12:7
Eph. 4:7
1 Pet. 4:10

Give to gain
Mt. 6:19-20
Lk. 6:38
2 Cor.9:6

Give to gain 2
Prov. 3:9-10
Prov. 11:25
Mal. 3:10

Give freely
Ex. 25:2
Ex. 35:29
2 Co. 9:7

Give things
Ex. 4:2
2 Ki. 4:2
Mt. 14:16

Goal
Phil. 2:16
1 Ts. 2:19-20
1 Jn. 2:28

Goal-city
Heb. 11:9-10
Heb. 11:16
Heb. 12:22-23

Goal-city 2
Heb. 13:13-14
Rev. 21:2
Rev. 21:9-10

God approves
Psa. 119:63
Lk. 9:49-50
Acts 10:34-35

God, faithful
Job. 23:10
Psa. 36:5
Psa. 89:1

God, faithful 2
Psa. 138:8
Psa. 146:5-6
Lam. 3:22

God, faithful 3
Isa. 40:28-29
1 Cor. 10:13
2 Ti. 2:13

God forgives
Eph. 1:7
1 Jn. 1:9
1 Jn. 2:1-2

God guides
Psa. 32:8
Prov. 3:5-6
Isa. 48:17

God in us
Eph. 3:20
Phil. 2:13
Col. 1:29

God invites
Isa. 1:18
Isa. 55:1
Ez. 33:11

God invites 2
Mt. 11:28-30
Jn. 6:37
Rev. 22:17

God is good
Rom. 8:28
Eph. 1:11
2 Ti. 1:8-9

God is true
Num. 23:18
Rom. 9:11
Eph.3:11

God keeps
Jn. 17:15
Gal. 1:3-4
Jude 1:24-25

God keeps 2
Rev. 3:10
Rev. 12:6
Rev. 12:14

God with us
Ex. 25:8
Jn. 1:14
Rev. 21:3

God's plan
Gen. 3:15
Gen. 12:3
Gen. 22:18

God's plan 2
Gen. 26:4
Gen. 28:14
Mt. 16:15

God's plan 3
Rom. 1:4-5
Eph. 1:10
1 Co.15:24-28

God's Promises
2 Cor. 1:20
Heb. 10:23
Heb. 11:11

God's Son
Mt. 3:17
Mt. 14:33
Mt. 16:16

God's Son, 2
Mt. 17:5
Mt. 27:43
Mt. 27:54

God's way?
Prov. 14:12
Isa. 55:8-9
Isa. 64:6

Godliness
1 Ti. 3:16
1 Ti. 4:7,8
1 Ti. 6:6-8

Good works
Eph. 2:10
Tit. 3:8
Heb. 10:24

Gospel
Rom. 1:18
1 Cor. 15:3-5
Gal. 1:8

Grace
1 Cor. 1:4-5
2 Cor. 9:8
1 Pet. 5:10

Heaven
Jn. 14:1-2
2 Cor. 5:1
2 Cor. 5:6-8

Heaven 2
Phil. 1:22
Rev. 21:4
Rev. 21:27

Hell
Psa. 9:17
Mt. 25:46
Lk. 16:23

Himself
Isa. 28:5
Isa. 28:12
Isa. 28:16

Holiness
Nu. 20:12-13
Isa. 5:16
Heb. 12:10-14

**Holy Spirit,
Ephesians**
Eph. 1:13-14
Eph. 4:1-2
Eph. 4:29-30

**Holy Spirit,
Ephesians 2**
Eph. 5:18-19
Eph. 6:17
Eph. 6:18

Homosexuals
Gen. 19:4-5
Rom. 1:26-27
1 Cor. 6:9-10

Hope
Rom. 5:2
Rom. 15:13
Cor. 1:27

Humility
Prov. 17:1-2
Isa. 57:15
Mt. 20:26-28

Humility 2
Phil. 2:3-4
Col. 3:12
1 Pet. 5:5-6

"I am"
Jn. 6:35
Jn. 8:12
Jn. 8:58

"I am" 2
Jn. 10:9
Jn. 10:11
Jn.14:6

Jesus: heart
Mt. 5:8
Mt. 12:34
Mt. 15:8-9

Jesus: heart 2
Mt. 15:18-20
Mt. 22:37-38
Mk. 7:21-23

Joy
Jn. 15:11
2 Cor. 6:10
Phil. 4:4

Judgment
Eccl. 12:14
Isa. 2:12
Dan. 7:9

Judgment 2
Heb. 9:;27
1 Pet. 4:17
Rev. 10:12

Judgment, Romans
Rom. 1:18
Rom. 2:12
Rom. 14:11-12

Kingdom
Dan. 2:44
Lk. 1:33
Rev. 11:15

Know God
1 Sam. 2:12
1 Sam. 3:7
Jer. 9:23-24

Know God 2
Mt. 7:22-23
Jn. 17:3
Phil. 3:8, 10

Knowledge
Prov. 15:2
Jas. 1:22
Jas. 4:17

Lamb
Gen. 22:7-8
Isa. 53:7
Jn. 1:29, 36

Lamb, 2
1 Pet. 1:18-19
Rev. 5:12
Rev. 13:8

Law / Christ
Rom. 7:4
Rom. 10:4
Gal. 5:4

Lawsuits
Prov. 25:8
Mt. 5:25-26
1 Cor. 6:7-8

Learn, How
Prov. 13:20
Prov. 14:6
Prov. 14:18

Life in Christ
2 Cor. 5:17
Col. 2:6
Col. 2:9-10

Life span
Psa. 39:4-5
Psa. 90:10
Psa. 92:13-14

Life, spiritual
Jn. 5:25
Jn. 10:10
1 Cor. 15:22

Life style
Lk. 6:40
Acts 2:46-47
1 Jn. 2:5-6

Life, Meaning
Acts 20:24
Acts 21:13
Acts 26: 28-29

Listen to God
Prov. 1:33
Prov. 8:34
Mt. 7:24-25

Live right
Eph. 4:1-3
Eph. 5:1-2
Eph. 5:8-9

Long view
Isa. 51:7-8
Isa. 51:12-13
Isa. 54:17

Lord, always
Acts 2:23-24
Acts 2:31-32
Acts 2:36

Love
Jn. 13:34-35
1 Cor. 13:4-7
Gal. 5:22

Love 2
Jas. 2:8
1 Jn. 3:23
1 Jn. 4:8

Love corrects
Lev. 19:17
Prov. 27:5
Mt. 18:15

Love people
Mt. 22:39
1 Cor. 3:17
1 Cor.13:1

Lust damns
Eph. 5:5
Heb. 13:4
Jas. 1:15

Lying, lethal
Jn. 8:44
Rev. 21:8
Rev. 21:27

**Mental
hygiene**
Eph. 5:12
Col. 3:16
Phil.4:8

Money, Get ?
Eccl. 5:10
1 Ti. 6:10
Heb. 13:5

Nature, new
Rom. 6:13
Rom. 8:11
2 Pet.1:4

Now/forever
1 Chr. 29:15
2 Cor. 4:18
1 Jn. 2:16-17

Obey
Rom. 5:19
Rom. 6:13
Rom. 12:1-2

Obey God
Jn. 14:21
Jn. 15:10,14
1 Jn. 2:3-4

Old vs. new
Rom. 6:6
Eph. 4:22-24
Col. 3:9-10

Our problem
Is. 1:5-6
Mk. 7:21-23
Rom. 3:10-12

"One thing"
Psa. 27:4
Lk. 10:41-42
Phil. 3:13

Omnipotence
Gen. 18:14
Job 42:2
Mt. 19:26

Omnipresence
Psa. 139:7
Jer. 23:23-24
Acts 17:27-18

Omniscience
Job 37:16
Psa. 147:5
1 Jn. 3:20

One sacrifice
Heb. 9:12
Heb. 9:26
Heb. 9:28

One sacrifice 2
Heb. 10:10
Heb.10:12-14
Heb. 10:17-18

OT timely
Lk. 4:4
Rom. 15:4
1 Co.10:11-12

Path of Light
Job 29:2-3
Prov. 4:18
Jn. 8:12

Patience
Heb. 10:36
Jas. 1:2-41
Pet.2:20

Paul: heart
Eph. 3:17
Eph. 5:18-19
Col. 3:16

Paul's preaching
Rom. 1:3-4
1 Cor. 2:2
Gal. 3:1

Peace
Jn. 14:27
Jn. 16:33
Phil. 4:6-7

People, Build
Acts 15:36
Col. 1:27-28
Gal. 3:1

Please God
2 Cor. 5:9
Col. 1:10
1 Ti. 4:1

Power
Eph. 1:18-19
Eph. 3:20
2 Ti. 1:7

Praise
Psa. 30:11-12
Psa. 34:6-7
Psa. 40:1-2

Prayer crippled
Psa. 66:18-19
Isa. 59:1-2
Mt. 5:23-24

Prayer crippled 2
Jas. 1:6-7
Jas. 4:2-3
1 Pet. 3:7

Pray often
Psa. 5:3
Psa. 55:17
Psa. 119:164

Pray often 2
Mk. 1:35
Lk. 18:1
1 Ts. 5:17-18

Prayers, Short
Neh. 2:4-5
Mt.14:30-31
Mt. 15:25

Prayer works
Jer. 33:3
Mt. 7:7-8
Lk. 18:7-8

Prayer works 2
Jn. 16:23
1 Jn. 3:22
1 Jn. 5:14-15

Preach
1 Cor. 1:23
1 Cor. 14:3
1 Ts. 2:11-12

Prosper
Jos. 1:8
Psa. 1:2-3
Psa. 19:9-11

Proverbs: heart
Prov. 4:23
Prov. 20:9
Prov. 23:26

Purpose, Life's
Jn. 10:10
Jn. 12:46
Jn. 19:37

Quarreling
Acts 24:15-16
2 Ti. 2::24-25
Jas. 1:19-20

Race
1 Cor. 9:24
2 Ti. 4:6-7
Heb. 12:1-2

Rapture
Jn. 14:3
1 Ts. 4:16-17
2 Ts. 2:1

Rebuke sin
Acts 5:3
Gal. 2:11
1 Ti. 5:20

Repent
Mt. 3:1-2
Mt. 4:17
Lk. 5:32

Repent 2
Lk. 13:3
Lk. 24:47-48
Acts 2:38

Resurrection
Mt. 12:39-40
Mt. 16:21
Mt. 17:9

Resurrection 2
Mt. 17:22-23
Mt. 20:18-19
Jn. 2:19-20

Resurrection 3
Rom. 6:4
Eph. 2:6-7
Col. 3:1

Revival
2 Chr. 7:14
Psa. 85:6
Hab. 3:2

Rewards
1 Cor. 15:58
2 Cor. 5:10
2 Ti. 4:8

Sabbath, sign
Ex. 31:12-13
Dt. 5:15
Ez. 20:12

**Sabbath,
temporary**
Acts 20:7
1 Cor. 16:2
Col. 2:16-17

Salvation, Free
Rom. 3:24
Eph. 2:8-9
Tit. 3:5

Satan's sons
Jn. 8:38
Jn. 8:41
Jn. 8:44

Satan's sons 2
1 Jn. 3:8
1 Jn. 3:12
1 Jn. 4:4

Satan's servants
2 Cor. 4:4
2 Co.11:13-14
Eph. 2:1-2

Saved for sure
1 Jn. 3:14
1 Jn. 5:11-12
1 Jn. 5:13

Savior, World
Jn. 4:42
1 Jn. 2:2
1 Jn. 4:14

Savior, Only
Mt. 11:27
Jn. 8:23-24
Jn. 14:6

Second coming
Mt. 24:42
Mk. 13:32
Jn. 14:2-3

Second coming 2
Rom. 13:12
Phil. 3:20
1 Ts. 4:16-27

Second coming 3
1 Ts. 5:2
Tit. 2:12-13
1 Jn. 3:1-2

Separate
Rom. 12:2
2 Cor. 6:17-18
1 Jn. 2:15-16

Servant foretold
Psa. 40:6-7
Isa. 11:1-2
Isa. 42:1-2

Shout
Psa. 95:1-3
Psa. 96:1-2
Psa. 98:4-5

Sin
Jn. 3:19
Rom. 3:10-12
Jas. 1:14-15

Sin destroys
Rom. 5:12
Rom. 6:23
Gal. 3:10

Son of God
Mt. 16:16
Mk. 14:61-62
Jn. 10:36

Son, supreme
Phil. 2:9-10
Col. 1:15-16
Heb. 1:1-3

**Sovereign
suffers**
Acts 2:23
Heb. 2:10
Rev. 5:12

Spirit exalts
Jn. 15:26
Jn. 16:14
1 Cor. 12:3

Spirit, honor
Isa. 44:3
Lk. 11:13
Acts 5:32

Spirit, Matt.
Mt. 3:11
Mt. 4:1
Mt. 12:28

Spirit, John
Jn. 3:34
Jn. 4:14
Jn. 7:37

Spirit, Life
Jn.3:5
2 Cor. 3:6
Tit. 3:5

"Stand"
Eph. 6:11
Eph. 6:13
Eph. 6:14

Strength
Eph. 3:14-16
Phil. 4:13
Col. 1:11-12

Success
Jos. 1:8
Psa. 1:2
Psa. 19:9-11

Suffer
Phil. 1:29
Heb. 12:3
1 Pet. 4:12-13

Teach
Mt. 28:19-20
Acts 17:2-3
1 Jn. 2:27

Thank you, Lord
Psa. 9:1-2
Psa. 18:48-19
Psa. 86:12-13

Things
Mt. 24:35
2 Pet. 3:10
1 Jn. 2:17

Tongue
Eph. 4:29
Jas. 1:26
Jas. 3:2

Tongue, bad
Psa. 141:3
Prov. 12:18
Prov. 17:27-30

Tribulation
Jn. 16:33
Acts 14:22
Rom. 8:35

Tribulation 2
2 Cor. 1:4
2 Ts. 1:6
Rev. 2:10

Unbelief
Jn. 3:18
Jn. 3:36
Jn. 8:23-24

Unbelief 2
Rom. 3:3
1 Jn. 5:10
Rev. 21:8

Use me, God
2 Chr. 16:9
Isa. 6:8
Ezek. 22:30

Victory
1 Cor. 10:13
2 Cor. 2:14
1 Jn. 5:4-5

Vows to God
Deut. 23:23
Psa. 76:11
Eccl. 5:4

Walk with God
Gen. 5:24
Gen. 17:1
Gen. 24:27

Warfare
Eph. 6:10-11
1 Ti. 6:11-12
2 Ti. 2:3-4

We, with Christ
Eph. 1:3
Eph. 2:6
Col. 3:1

Wife, godly
Prov. 18:22
Prov. 19:14
Prov. 31:30

Will of God
Mk. 3:35
Rom. 12:2
Eph. 5:17

Wisdom
1 Cor. 1:21
1 Cor. 1:30
Jas. 1:5

With Him
Mk. 3:14
Acts 16:3
2 Pet. 1:18

Witness
Mt. 4:19
Mt. 10:32-33
Mt. 16:15-16

Witness 2
Lk. 24:47-48
Jn. 9:25
Acts 1:8

Witness 3
2 Cor. 5:19-20
1 Ts. 1:8
1 Ti. 4:16

Witness 4
1 Pet. 3:14-15
1 Jn. 1:1-2
Rev.12:11

Witness
always
Prov. 10:5
Eccl. 11:4
2 Ti. 4:2

Worldly cares
Mt. 13:22
Mk. 4:18-19
Lk. 21:34

World vision
Mt. 3:38
Mt. 24:14
Mt. 26:13

World vision 2
Mk. 16:15
Jn. 3:16-17
Col. 1:6

Wrath of God
Psa. 90:11
Jer. 10:24
Lam. 2:22

Wrath of God 2
Ezek. 7:19
Rom. 1:18
Rev. 14:10

Homegrown Themes

The themes and texts you have memorized are the Bible foundation of your faith—Granite! Another way to add themes is to discover them yourself as you read the Bible.

You can "grow" Bible themes as a fruit of your regular times in the Word. While reading the Bible a text suddenly grabs your attention. You say, "Wow! I never saw *that* before, I've got to remember *that*." But how?

In a loose-leaf notebook title a page, "Theme Seedbed." When a text startles you, open to that page, then ask, "Why did that text grip me? What does it say? Why do I want to remember it?" Then, write that theme in your Seedbed.

To keep your themes in approximate alphabetic order for convenience, note three letters per sheet, A, B, C, etc. As a page in your Theme Seedbed fills up, copy its content on a new sheet. With a computer this exercise is easier and quicker.

Take Acts 5:32, for example. It has two themes at least, "Obedience" and "Holy Spirit." Write those words under "O" and "H" with "Acts 5:32" beside each.

As you read your Bible you will find other texts that deepen your understanding of "obedience" or "Holy Spirit". Write each reference in your seedbed beside the appropriate theme, or if new, add the theme.

Do the same with any text you find that relates to a theme you already have, or a new theme you want to develop. Building themes will add a new dimension to your Bible reading.

My rule is to require three texts on any theme to qualify it to be memorized.

Also be sure to record in a notebook every homegrown theme and its texts that you memorize. Should you lose your Daily Pack you will be thankful for that record.

Tribute: Daily Pack

My joy to have with me always;
My blessing when away from home;
My help to be an obedient witness;
My aid in "redeeming the time;"
My admission of hunger to walk with God;
My companion in quiet moments;
My conversation piece when appropriate;
My container of timeless Truth;
My testimony as a card-carrying believer;
My guardian against lost time;
My flag "nailed to the mast" for Truth;
My badge of allegiance to Christ;
My reminder to prepare for heaven;
My faith-builder for life's final test.
Forget the pictures that don't make sense,
Remember the ones you like the best
—NL

Tremendous Tool

To memorize and meditate Bible texts you will need a case to carry theme and text cards. If you carry the cards unprotected they soon wear out. A Daily Pack is the answer.

The best, most durable material for a Daily Pack is the vinyl used to cover car seats. The trim that auto upholsterers produce as a by-product of their work is very durable. It is easy to sew, will last a lifetime and can often be had for little or no cost.

Tightly woven cloth, though less durable than vinyl, also works well. It is easy to obtain and to sew.

It is good to have extra card cases for others who may follow your example, hiding the Word of God in their hearts. You have been blessed by memorizing Scripture in order to be a blessing to others. (See Genesis 12:3). Others, seeing your example will want to imitate you.

Also, you may lose a card case. My Daily Pack was taken by a pickpocket in Morocco as I boarded a crowded train. A similar loss occurred in Lima, Peru, on a bus with standing room only.

The thieves were probably disgusted when they saw the cards instead of cash, but the texts may have done them good. A third pack was lost on a deer hunt in the U.S. Three Daily Packs lost in 63 years, however, is not a bad record.

Should your Daily Pack be lost or stolen, you have only to rewrite the lost cards and replace the case. So, in order to be consistent with your long-term plan to memorize and meditate the Bible, be wise and make extra cases.

Record in a notebook any theme and its texts you learn from a source other than this book as a back-up if you should lose your Daily Pack.

Desire to use God's Word in witnessing and your need to review daily make the Daily Pack important. Remember, to hide God's Word in your heart is not a short race. Rather, it is a marathon that demands endurance. "Use them or lose them" is true of the texts you learn.

That is why you are told on the next page how to make a Daily Pack.

Make a Pack

Diagram is NOT drawn to scale.
Follow measurements given below.

- - - - - - - - - - - - - (fold here) - - - - - - - - - - - - - -

Pattern: Cut a rectangle of vinyl or cloth 20.5 centimeters long (8 inches), by 11cm. wide (4 1/4 inches).

Cards are 9.5 cm. long (3 3/4 inches), by 5.9 cm. wide (2 1/4 inches).

Fold 3 cm. (1 1/4 inches) from both ends at dotted lines to the solid lines at 6 cm. (2 1/2 inches) from each end.

Sew firmly along one edge. Before sewing other edge, test with 16 cards to be sure they fit loosely in the pocket.

━━━━━━━━━━━━(center fold)━━━━━━━━

A loose fit is important to make it easy to remove and replace cards.

A vinyl Pack will never wear out; cloth is next best. Always carry cards with you for frequent review.

Your Daily Pack will hold up to 32 cards, 16 in each pocket.

Fold Pack in the middle, along heavy, solid line.

- - - - - - - - - - - - - (fold here) - - - - - - - - - - - - - -

Daily Pack, Open

Read to Obey

D.L. Moody was an outstanding, influential evangelist during the second half of the 19th century. His illustrations were remembered and repeated by people of all classes. Moody speaks to the importance of Bible reading.

"I used at one time to read so many chapters of the Bible a day, and if I did not get through my usual quantity, I thought I was getting cold and back sliding. But, mind you, if a man had asked me two hours afterward what I had read, I could not tell him; I had forgotten it nearly all.

"When I was a boy, I used, among other things, to hoe corn on the farm; and I used to hoe it so badly, in order to get over so much ground, that at night I had to put down a stick in the ground so as to know next morning where I had left off.

"That was somewhat in the same fashion as running through so many chapters every day. A man will say, 'Wife, did I read that chapter?'

'Well,' says she, 'I don't remember.'"

"And neither of them can recollect. And perhaps he read the same chapter over and over again; and they call that 'studying the Bible.'"

"I do not think there is a book in the world we neglect so much as the Bible."[13]

Could Moody charge us with careless Bible reading today? If so, we are insulting God. Let us repent of our lazy habits by building into our daily schedules more time with God's Word.

"Oh, how I love Your law! It is my meditation all the day" (Psa. 119:97). Feeding my body may have to be done in less time to help me focus on feeding my spirit.

Obey God! Feed your spirit more than your body. Say with Job, "I have not departed from the commandment of His lips. I have esteemed the words of His mouth more than my necessary food" (Job 23:12). Build your immortal spirit

John Wesley, a witness

Another hero of our biblical faith who strongly advocated daily Bible reading was John Wesley, founder of the Methodist Church.

Wesley said, "Do not hastily ascribe things to God. Do not easily suppose dreams, impressions, voices, visions, or revelations to be from God. They may be from Him. They may be from nature. They may be from the Devil...

"Try all things by the written Word, and let all bow down before it. You are in danger...every hour, if you depart ever so little from the Scripture; yes, or from the plain, literal meaning of any text taken in connection with the context."

Wesley also emphasized that a way to let error in is "expecting knowledge, for instance, without searching the Scriptures... Some have been ignorant of this device of Satan. They have left off searching the Scriptures. They said, 'God writes all the Scriptures on my heart. Therefore I have no need to read it.'"[14]

God's Word also warns us against false sources of truth so-called: "I have heard what the prophets have said who prophesy lies in My name, saying, 'I have dreamed, I have dreamed!' How long will this be in the heart of the prophets who prophesy lies? Indeed they are prophets of the deceit of their own heart, who try to make My people forget My name by their dreams which everyone tells his neighbor, as their fathers forgot My name for Baal" (Jer. 23:25-).

With people everywhere exposed to secular humanism and materialism, it should not surprise us that many who call themselves believers live as practical atheists. That erosion of faith is widespread even in areas where the Bible has long been available.

What can be done to escape that danger? The answer is plain. Believers of all ages must repent of their neglect of God's Word and drink daily at that fountain. The Bible is given us to read, memorize, meditate and obey. Wesley emphatically exalted God's Word.

"Is not My word like a fire?" says the Lord, "And like a hammer that breaks the rock in pieces" (Jer. 23:29)? We must saturate ourselves with the Bible until we become obedient, godly people.

Alexander Whyte, a witness

Rev. John Kelman, an intimate of Dr. Alexander Whyte's, said of Whyte that he "was an extraordinary man, unlike anyone else one ever saw. He was one of the very few men of our generation, or for that matter, of any other generation, concerning whom every one must agree that they were men of sheer genius.

"Some such men appear in quiet places, and their genius discovers itself only to one here and there who may chance to push back the leaves and find it in the lowly and concealing grass. Others, of whom he was one, find themselves in positions which proclaim their genius to the ends of the earth and far and near 'stir the great minds of men.'"

Dr. Whyte said:

"The complete and finished Book of God, Old Testament and New, has been delivered to us to see what we will make of it. To see how we will search it, and what we will find in it, and in ourselves by means of it, and then all that will infallibly decide what we are and what we will make of ourselves, and where we will find ourselves at last.

"All the other books in this wide world taken together do not for one moment concern us in comparison with this Book.

"For the whole meaning and purpose and true end and design of our existence, as of our Lord's existence; all our Maker's purpose and intention in our creation, preservation, and redemption; our chief end on earth, and our endless enjoyment of God in heaven—all that is here, and is nowhere else."[15]

What a weighty appeal to read the Bible daily, ambitiously while life lasts. Dr. Whyte's words go deep. Arguably, they are more needed today than when they were written.

Whyte says the Bible "has been delivered to us to see what we will make of it." We are responsible. "For we must all stand before Christ to be judged. We will each receive whatever we deserve for the good or evil we have done in our bodies" (2 Cor. 5:10). Do we really think our obedience through reading God's Word will shelter us from God's judgment?

Author, a witness

A man "embarrassed" me into reading the Bible. God's grace did it, no credit to me. Seven years had passed since my conversion. The members of the small church responsible for my receiving Christ had made me their pastor. Of course I "preached the Bible," but had never read it all.

Then Rev. John Linton came from Canada for special meetings. His sermons were powerful. One evening after the service a small group gathered around him.

During a pause I asked, "How can I study the Bible to get messages like you preach?" Linton was quiet, his gray eyes probing mine, then he asked, "Have you ever read the Bible, all of it?" I was trapped. To admit I had not before my people? Never!

I mouthed something about favorite Bible portions and turned to slink away. Then came the bombshell. "You will never understand the Bible till you have read it from cover to cover at least thirty times."

That crushing word would change my life. Read the Bible from cover to cover thirty times? I had never even thought of such a goal. I thought hard as I drove home alone that night. Did it make sense? I decided it did? Was the challenge for me? I knew it was!

The next morning I counted pages in my Bible and did some arithmetic. Then I read seven chapters from Genesis (OT) and two from Matthew (NT). My aim was to finish both testaments in six months, on the same day if possible. It looked tough, but Linton's words had moved me to the core.

It took me about 180 days to finish the Bible once, and about the same the second time through. Each time my resolve increased. Twice I read it all five times in a year. The result? Heart response! Excitement! Vision! Blessing! The Bible came alive, searched me, convicted me.

Yes, God stands behind His incredible Word. That is one reason for this book. Others need to know. But for now, focus on your own life. The Bible reveals what God wants from you. Let God speak. Read: Jos. 1:8, Psa. 1:2-3, Psa. 19:9-11, Dt. 6:6-7, Lk. 4:4, Heb. 4:12. Ask yourself, "Am I obeying God?" If not, "Am I willing to cast myself on His mercy, and obey Him?"

Read God's Word Daily

1. Ask a commitment from your pastor and an elder to hold you accountable. Promise them and God that from now on you will read the Bible at least forty minutes a day (more is better, but 40 is the number of testing), in order to obey God;

2. When? If you can, start with God first every day, before your mind is filled with the day's concerns;

3. Feed in both testaments daily. If you read 3 1/2 pages of the Old Testament and 1 page of the New Testament daily, you will finish the Bible (in most versions) in less than a year;

4. If you deeply "hunger and thirst for righteousness" as Jesus put it, (Mt. 5:6), you can set a higher mark. You might read 7 pages OT and 2 pages NT daily. But it is better to achieve a modest goal than to set your sights too high and fail;

5. Measure readings by pages, which are uniform. Stop at the end of the first chapter after your daily page quota. On a calendar mark book and chapter where you finish each day. A month before you finish, adjust readings to end both testaments the same day. Next day start Genesis and Matthew.

6. If you don't finish your daily reading, make it up that day. Be strict, the prize is huge! "Whatever you do will prosper." Reread "Life-Success Promise," page 39.

7. Fill out and sign the following agreement. Ask your pastor and an elder to sign your "Covenant with God" as witnesses. They will help you.

"Each Word"

For several years I read the whole Bible twice every twelve months. It is a great and powerful tree, each word of which is a mighty branch. Each of these branches I have shaken.

—*Martin Luther*

Covenant with God

I believe that the mighty promise of God to Joshua (Jos. 1:8) is trustworthy; and that similar promises in Psalm 1:2-3, and in Psalm 19:9-11, extend God's promise to anyone who will meet God's condition.

God does not show favoritism (Rom. 2:11, 3:22-23, 10:12-13).

I commit myself to read the Bible ambitiously every morning in both testaments as a permanent covenant with God in order to obey Him.

If an emergency causes me to break my promise to God, I will do the missed reading later that day, or as soon as I possibly can. I will not excuse myself even when the going gets tough, but will count on God's grace to sustain me. My prayer today and always will be, for strength to be true to my covenant with You, my Lord and my God.

_____
Signature   Date

_____
Pastor   Date

_____
Elder   Date

"A threefold cord is not quickly broken"
(Eccl. 4:12).

This Book and You

This book tells how God led me to obey Him. He asks obedience of us all. My life to university years was ordinary. My parents were neither rich nor poor. My siblings, three brothers and a sister were normal. The outdoors was my love, hunting and fishing.

But early in my pre-med studies at the University of Nebraska the claims of Christ got me. I was converted. The group through which Christ found me was missions-minded. The Bible convinced me that all followers of Christ were responsible to make disciples among all nations. That conviction has stayed with me. To believe God makes one a missionary at heart.

Less than a year after my conversion a failure in witnessing (see page 41) thrust me into Scripture memorizing using cards to review chosen texts. It made me ask myself what the text before me was really saying. This became a life-focus for me.

Six years later I was "embarrassed" into reading the whole Bible (see page 88). A visiting pastor, in answer to my question said, "You will never understand the Bible until you have read it from cover to cover at least thirty times." That crushing statement would change my life. It pushed me into the Bible to understand it, a quest that for sixty two years has been like swimming in an ocean of light.

Over fifty years later another light from God's Word shined on me. It was the idea that reading the Bible, God's unique manna for our spiritual growth, deserves more time than feeding our body.

The logic is simple. The body is temporary. It will soon return to dust. The spirit is eternal. God's children through faith in Christ will spend forever with Him (see Jn. 14). The body deserves excellent care. The care of the spirit is even more important..

The huge imbalance between believers' care of body and spirit has had tragic results.We are consumed by soulish and physical things. Our culture poisons us with the notion that the Bible and obedience to God are minor matters (see page 25).

The remedy is radical. Repent; about face. Read, memorize, and meditate God's Word in a way that fits deep repentance. Is your heart open? Then do this. Read the Bible to start the day (see pages 85-90). Use time at noon to review texts and add new ones (see pages 37-68). In the evening read more Bible and meditate it. Live to obey God. He will answer you in revolutionary ways.

Life Plan

Whether you have only skimmed this book, or find your copy worn from use, please consider the significance of its message in God's plan. The Bible, like its Author, is awesome.

What is the Bible to you? You may not yet be convinced that to obey God will guarantee you success, although that is what God's Word says. True, to believe God risks a lot on faith. Perhaps He planned it that way.

The self-revealing I Am tells us that "Without faith it is impossible to please Him, for he who comes to God must believe that He is, and that He is the rewarder of those who diligently seek Him" (Heb. 11:6).

Will you live all out for Jesus Christ? Will you put your faith completely in Him? It's up to you. His wide promise includes you. God has made your decision to read the Bible with the aim to obey Him the condition of his prospering you in all you do.

When humanity's existence on planet earth has become history, the challenge to you through this encounter with truth may be printed on the canvas of your memory as a watershed decision that determined your destiny.

The truth in this book will be confirmed in the day when all things are revealed. Fulfill the condition and what will occur? It will be proved in that hour that God is truth. His word is true. That is fact, ultimate reality! How important it will be then, beyond words now to exaggerate, to learn that God's grace gave you a part in vindicating His righteousness.

To read Old and New Testaments daily, to memorize and meditate the Bible in order to obey God, has enabled countless believers, like Enoch, to "walk with God" (Gen. 5:24), and like Paul, to "fight the good fight of faith" and to "lay hold on eternal life" (1 Tim. 6:12). So feed your spirit as often and more carefully than your body. God has kept his promise through all the ages to people who come to Him in faith (see Heb.11:6 above). He will continue to do so.

Comments, criticisms, or other response, are invited by the author who can be reached through the publishers.

Sources

1.*Huston* : James M. Huston Editor, *The Mind On Fire*, Multnomah Press, Portland, OR, 1989, p. 11

2. *Pascal :* Blaise Pascal, *Pensees and The Provincial Letters,* Random House, New York 1941

3. *Cable and French,* Mildred Cable and Francesca French, *The Bible in Mission Lands.* Fleming H. Revell Company, London and Edinburgh, 1947, p. 18
   The authors were missionaries of CIM (now Overseas Missionary Fellowship). After years in North China they became pioneer missionaries in the Gobi Desert. They have been awarded both the Lawrence of Arabia and the Livingstone medals and have written many books.

4. *Bunyan:* John Bunyan, *The Pilgrim's Progress,* Barbour and Company, Inc., 164 Mill Street, Westwood, NJ, p. 42

5. *Gaebelein*: Frank E. Gaebelein, Editor, *A Christianity Today Reader,* Article, "The Book That Understands Me", 11/22/63, Meredith Press, New York, p.14
   Cailliet wrote, "In the beginning God..." the four opening words of our Bible constitute the charter for all sound thinking. It is not enough to rely on the genius answers uncovered from past experience, or on the great scientific advance of our own age for the solution to our problems...
   The way to sanity and to a genuine knowledge and understanding of the world of nature and of man is to take into account the entire landscape of reality and to survey it in the light of Scripture. *Cailliet ,* Emile Cailliet, preface to *The Christian Approach to Culture,* Abingdon-Cokesbury Press, New York, 1953.

6. *Barnhouse:* Donald Grey Barnhouse, *Christianity Today*

7. *MacArthur:* John MacArthur, Jr.,*Our Sufficiency in Christ,* Word Publishing, Dallas, TX, 1939, p. 88

8. *Busse-Grawitz:* Irma Busse-Grawitz, Sanatorio Diquecito, Cordoba, Argentina, Letter to author.

(continued)

9. *Byron:* Dr. Ralph Byron, *Surgeon of Hope,* Fleming H. Revell Company, Old Tappan, NJ, p. 11

10. *Swindoll:* Charles R. Swindoll, *Growing Strong in the Seasons of Life*, Multnomah Press, Portland, OR 1983, p. 53

11. *Keilhacker:* Rose Keilhacker, Testimony

12. *Perez*: Linda Perez, letter from Linda Perez' pastor to author.

13. *Lundin and Noll:* Roger Lundin and Mark Noll, Editors *Voices From the Heart,* Erdmans, 1987, p. 215

14. *Whaling*: Frank Whaling Editor, *John and Charles Wesley,* Paulist Press, New York, 1981, p. 237

15. *Turnbull:* Ralph G. Turnbull, Editor,*The Treasury of Alexander Whyte,* Baker House, Grand Rapids, MI 1953, p. 205

16. Barbour, *George F Barbour, Alexander Whyte,* Hodder and Stoughton Ltd., New York, 1923

The words quoted from Dr. Alexander Whyte are so focused and severe that we are left wondering what the man himself was like. The 675 page biography of Whyte by Barbour helps one to visualize the man.

For example, minutes before a meeting in his church, with several men, Dr. Whyte asked one of them to lead in prayer. As he did so the man prayed especially that the Spirit of Love might rule in their midst. Then, as the men left the room, Dr. Whyte spoke in a tone so low that only the friend who had prayed could hear, "You asked for the loving heart, but you've got it!"

A similar encouragement is in a four word phrase in a note to one who had long been a member of his church, "When you are near God, as you always are, sometimes remember me and mine."

As pastor, he visited one who had suffered much and whose heart was nearly broken. He knelt with her in her poor room and said simply, "Oh Lord, here's two poor old folk needing you sorely. You won't be hard on us!" He was humble, having drunk deeply at the Bible fountain.

17. Segalini, *Erik Segalini,Worldwide Challenge*, "Shields and Swords, Sept./Oct. 1998, Vol. 25, Nu. 5, page 23

Index

96